T0008497

The Little Book *of* Crystal Magic

Also by Sarah Bartlett

The Little Book of Practical Magic
The Little Book of Moon Magic
The Little Book of Earth Magic

The Little Book *of* Crystal Magic

Sarah Bartlett

PIATKUS

PIATKUS

First published in Great Britain in 2022 by Piatkus

1 3 5 7 9 10 8 6 4 2

A CIP catalogue record for this book is available from the British Library.

ISBN 978-0-3494-3037-9

Typeset in Perpetua by M Rules
Printed and bound in Great Britain by Clays Ltd, Elcograf S.p.A.

Papers used by Piatkus are from well-managed forests and other responsible sources.

Piatkus
An imprint of
Little, Brown Book Group
Carmelite House
50 Victoria Embankment
London EC4Y 0DZ

An Hachette UK Company
www.hachette.co.uk

www.littlebrown.co.uk

To Jess, and all who care for this Planet Earth

Acknowledgments

My thanks go to everyone at Piatkus for helping to make this little book such a magical one, and all the people involved in its creation at Little, Brown and Hachette.

I would also like to thank my daughter, Jess, for contributing her frog illustration, and my friends, the crystals, who inspired me to write this book.

Contents

PART THREE

Magic Spells, Rituals, Charms and Practices

PART FOUR

Crystal Protection and Healing

PART FIVE

Crystal Divination

Introduction

My first encounter with magical stones was on a pebble beach in southern England when I was in my twenties. I'd just been through a break-up, and as I sat gazing out to sea, wondering how I'd get over it, I idly picked up a pebble that had washed up on the shore. Formed by a million years or so of life at sea, its perfect oval shape felt warm and protective in my hand. As I looked more closely at the black, smooth stone that had befriended me, I saw that it was etched with two fine grey lines at each end: perhaps a hint that some creature had attached itself to that stone thousands of years ago. To me, it was a sign from the universe, as if this small stone held all of eternity in its atomic lattice. In that moment, I understood how to let go of the past and live for the present.

No matter how well you describe it, this kind of feeling must be experienced personally to fully understand it. Somehow, I was truly in touch with the energy of the universe as it permeated all things, including pebbles, rocks, the ocean and human beings. The stone is still with me in a special place in my home, and since then I have befriended other crystals and stones, either through choice or by chance, but always due to the magic workings of the universe.

This book is a tribute to the magic of crystals and will enable you to connect to the innate power within you, too.

Harnessing a million years of energy

The mysterious aura that crystals exude has entranced humanity for thousands and thousands of years. It's not only the energy radiating from them, but also their practical or spiritual significance: their enigmatic beauty has inspired legends and mysteries, while many signify wealth and riches. Revered as priceless gems, protective talismans and healing stones, their magic lies both in their tangible attraction and their numinous connection to the universe. In fact, crystals have been – and still are – empowering tools for all kinds of self-help, healing, protection and divination. To hold a crystal is to hold a million years or so of Earth energy in your hands, and that is nature's magic indeed.

This little book covers all kinds of crystal magic, from simple beneficial practices, spells and rituals, to creating empowerment grids and protection for your home and family. You will also learn how to use crystals to divine your needs, desires and future choices, helping you live the life you want.

Throughout this book, I often refer to crystals as 'stones'. To me, a stone is as precious as any rare gem or crystal. However, to define and understand the origins of the technical term 'crystal', and to distinguish it from the wild stones I also use later in the book, let's begin by looking at where 'crystals' originate.

PART ONE

Discovering Crystals and Sacred Stones

In this section you'll discover everything you need to know about the origins, traditions and uses of crystals, as well as how to buy, choose and care for your stones. We'll also explore ways to find and connect to wild stones, which are just as important as the crystals you buy. The aim is to equip you with all the knowledge you need to start building your own collection.

Chapter One

Fact and Mystique

The life of a crystal starts deep within the Earth's crust. Although the planet appears solid and stable, beneath the surface, it is in constant motion due to the effects of its rotational orbit around the sun, not forgetting the gravitational influences of the moon and the other planets. The apparently solid rock upon which we live is actually a thin 'skin' covering a turbulent interior. Within the Earth's mantle are massive layers of rock that are actually moving plates. Depending on external influences, these constantly shift, sliding across one another, at times creating unwanted phenomena such as volcanoes and earthquakes.

Magma

All this stress creates fractures in the Earth's crust, and, under extreme pressure, hot gases, liquids and molten rock known as magma are forced up into the fissures and rise towards the surface. As the magma moves upwards, various elements and minerals, such as water, sodium, gold or iron, permeate it. As it passes through cooler layers, it begins to crystallise in caverns or underground hollows, and depending on the environment and mix of elements and minerals, gemstones and crystals will form. The time this takes varies: amethyst, for example, takes hundreds of years to develop, while obsidian forms in a matter of days.

Common characteristics

When minerals or elements form into crystals, they all have fundamentally the same arrangement of atoms, reflected in the geometric shapes we see in their facets and angles. Uncannily, crystals are, in a sense, alive, and they do grow. Depending on the conditions, small crystals grow in the form of geodes, the main source of stones such as amethyst and banded agates. The colour in crystals is due to small impurities in minerals such as magnesium, calcium, sodium or iron, or other elements within the structure. So don't assume all topaz is pale blue, or that all opal is iridescent white. There are a variety of different-coloured tourmalines, agates and quartz crystals too.

Crystal vibration and energy

We often take crystals for granted, perhaps not realising how useful they have been to mankind. They are used as major components in everything from the well-known quartz watch to satellites and other complex machinery; they are also used to make pigments for dyes and paints, as well as being utilised in chemicals and medicines. They even feature in our diet as the salt we eat. Their orderly arrangement of atoms is the most stable form of matter in the universe, and their unique vibrational energy comes from this solid, repetitive atomic pattern or lattice.

Vibration

French physicist and chemist Pierre Curie (1859–1906) discovered something called the 'piezoelectric effect' in crystals. In simple terms, when mechanical stress is applied to a crystal – for instance, by squeezing it – a voltage is produced across the crystal's surface. This is how quartz watches work.

If you hold a crystal tightly in your hand, you will feel it warm up. What you are doing is applying stress to the crystal so that its electromagnetic force comes alive which produces a vibrational resonance.

If we align our own intentions to the different vibrational energies of individual crystals (usually indicated by their colour), we can use this vibrational energy to boost and reinforce our desires. For example, we can use the 'low' vibrational field of obsidian (black) to help us have a reliable, consistent home life, or we can make a crystal grid with high vibrational citrine (yellow) to attract abundance.

Ways to use crystals

From magic spells to protection grids, from chakra-healing to casting crystal oracles, there are many wondrous and magical ways you can use crystals.

Magic

For thousands of years, stones and crystals have been used as amulets and talismans, adorning pharaohs, accompanying the dead to the afterlife, and bringing wealth to kings and queens. By incorporating crystals into rituals and spells, you can connect to the universal magic within you, as well as using protective talismans or amulets to manifest your desires and keep you safe. You can practise natural magic, and recite incantations or verses that will connect you with crystal energies and powers, invoking beneficial influences to help you achieve your goals.

Protection

Due to the electromagnetic energy of crystals, they can be used to protect you from the negative psychic energy of others, or simply from the geopathic stress around you (we'll look at this in more detail in chapter 8). Dark crystals, such as black tourmaline, obsidian and smoky quartz, can be placed in your home to absorb negative energy. You can also wear or carry crystals such as amber, black jade or pyrite to protect you from the polluted energy of others, such as rival colleagues or a difficult partner, or even the jostling energy exuding from an entire crowd of people. Wearing amber will protect you from projected envy or the toxic thoughts of others, while carrying fluorite will guard you from general geopathic stress in the environment.

Healing

Many types of healing practices, both physical and spiritual, incorporate crystals. For example, crystals can be placed on different parts of your body to balance your chakra energies (see below), or they can be used for spiritual healing, helping you to gain awareness of your deeper self. Certain crystals, such as amethyst, selenite and moonstone, will help you meditate, and in yoga, surrounding your mat with choice quartz will enable you to flow smoothly into your poses and restore the dynamics of your body. There is a wide range of crystal grids you can place around your home to boost your well-being, enhance your emotions or improve your general psychological health. For instance, a red garnet grid improves sexual energy levels and alleviates emotional disharmony, while one of brown jasper stimulates the immune system and calms an overactive mind.

The chakras

The chakras (a Sanskrit word meaning 'wheels') are likened to epicentres of invisible energy that are believed to flow around and through the body. These vibrate at different electromagnetic frequencies, forming an ephemeral interface or channel between our personal energy and that of the cosmos. The chakras also correspond to the vibrational frequencies of the seven colours of the rainbow, and these, in turn, are traditionally associated with seven gemstones. There are seven main chakras: the crown; the brow or third eye; the throat; the heart; the solar plexus; the sacral; and the root or base. Each chakra aligns to certain functions and qualities within us.

- Crown chakra crystal: clear quartz
- Brow or third eye chakra crystal: amethyst
- Throat chakra crystal: lapis lazuli
- Heart chakra crystal: emerald
- Solar plexus chakra crystal: citrine
- Sacral chakra crystal: red carnelian
- Root or base chakra crystal: ruby

We will explore working with chakras in more detail in chapter nine.

Divination

Because their vibrational power connects them to the universe, crystals can be used as a channel for cosmic knowledge from the past, present and future. You can 'divine' or 'read' the future by placing crystals in special layouts as you might do with tarot cards, or by casting them on a zodiac board to reveal what needs attention in your life right now. Most crystals correspond or vibrate to the symbolic essence of the celestial bodies, and can be laid out in various geometrical designs to promote the qualities associated with a particular planet. Crystals can be interpreted as oracles, taken from a pouch and used as a guide for what sort of day you might have. You can also use a dowsing crystal to help you find lost objects or make important decisions for the future. We'll look at divination in more detail in part five.

Medicinal healing

Using crystals to heal a medical or physical condition requires training, practice or the consultation of a qualified therapist. Crystals can be placed on various points around the body to calm or vitalise physical symptoms, but it is only advisable to do this after seeking professional advice.

Mystique

Since ancient times, there have been legends concerning the healing and magical powers of crystals: ancient Greek sibyls divined the future by casting dazzling quartz on to obsidian mirrors; medieval apothecaries distilled love elixirs from garnets; Renaissance witches used bloodstones to influence the weather; and gold rings set with mystical toadstones were worn by royalty to protect them from poisoners.

Here are a few examples of crystal-based legends and folklore from around the world.

Ancient Babylon

Well over six thousand years ago, the ancient Babylonians believed that crystals were placed on Earth as gifts from the planetary gods they worshipped. They used crystals in magic formulas and spells, and to predict the future, believing each stone was filled with the energy of specific planetary gods. The Sumerian myth of Gilgamesh describes a mystic cedar tree bearing lapis lazuli fruits and flowers. Another text describes how the solar god, Ninib, blessed some stones and cursed others: the god favoured alabaster for building work, but chalcedony angered him, and so it was doomed to be never used within any structure. In Assyrian culture, there were two curious stones that were worn as talismans by the elite, known as the 'Stone of Non-Love' and the 'Stone of Love'. Although it is not recorded exactly which crystals these were, when worn on the body, they would bestow the wearer with either the quality of passionate love or that of zealous hate.

Ancient Egypt and Greece

The ancient Egyptians used crystals lavishly for decoration, as jewellery and as funerary items to aid the dead on their journey to the afterlife. Favoured stones for amulets and talismans were lapis lazuli, carnelian, hematite and green jasper. According to a fragment of a fourth-century BCE Greek lapidary (a text about the properties of precious and semi-precious stones), a specific collection of protective amulets was given to sailors before they set sail: chalcedony protected the sailor from drowning; aquamarine banished fear; fire agate protected against the Evil Eye; while coral was attached to the prow of the ship to guard against dangerous winds, waves and storms. Banded agate was also carried to prevent fear of the surging swells of the ocean, and lastly jet protected the owner from all evil deeds when on the vessel.

Classical and medieval

From classical antiquity right through to the end of the medieval period, the lodestone (magnetite) was believed to have extraordinary magical power. Legend tells how the lodestone was discovered on Mount Ida by a shepherd named Magnes, when his iron-nail-encrusted shoes stuck to a piece of the rock. One fifth-century CE Roman poet recounts how temple priests carved two statues: one of Venus, carved out of lodestone; and the other of Mars, carved out of iron. The two statues were placed close to one another at a marriage feast and the lodestone magically drew the iron statue towards it. According to medieval European folklore, if the stone was placed under the pillow of a sleeping wife, it would reveal her virtue. If she embraced her husband in the night, she was faithful; if she got out of bed, she had already strayed.

With the rise of Hermetic philosophy, esotericism

and alchemy in the Renaissance period, gemstones were thought to possess more magical power than anything else in the cosmos. The mysterious alchemical and Hermetic text known as the *Emerald Tablet* was said to have been written by the legendary figure Hermes Trismegistus on a huge emerald. In his work *Hermetica*, the humanist philosopher Marsilo Ficino elaborated on these beliefs around gemstones, saying that stones such as rubies, quartz crystal, emeralds and sapphires could do miraculous things, such as resist fire, divert lightning, endow wisdom, repel poison and increase riches.

Christianity and royal courts

For the Christian church, the significance of precious stones lay more in their intrinsic value rather than any beliefs around their powers. However, an apocryphal story tells of how Saint Valentine wore an amethyst ring with a mythological Cupid engraved upon it, revealing his acceptance of classical mythology. Meanwhile, the royal courtiers of Europe were obsessed with wearing toadstone rings to ward off would-be poisoners. Toadstones, also known as bufonites, were actually the button-shaped fossilised teeth of lepidotes, an ancient kind of fish. At the time, though, it was widely believed that these magical stones were found in the heads of toads. Set in rings as anti-venom devices, or used as cures for anything from kidney ailments to epilepsy, it was believed that if the stone changed colour, it revealed toxic people or poisoners were nearby.

By the Renaissance period, royal courts were filled

with sorcery, alchemical intrigue and witchy plots, and potions, poisons, crystals and perfumes were essential ingredients in any shrewd apothecary's shop. Catherine de Medici, who was heavily into all things esoteric and dabbled in magic herself, wore a girdle set with twelve precious stones corresponding to each of the zodiac signs. Engraved with talismans and mystical symbols, the girdle was worn as a protective amulet against witchcraft – not forgetting those conspirators who prowled the French royal chateaux and courts looking to bring down the Catholic monarchy.

Far East

By far the most prized and popular stone in China and the Far East is jade, which can refer to two different minerals, nephrite and jadeite. In Chinese culture, jade jewellery was given to girls when they came of age to ensure they had a happy future marriage. In eighteenth-century China, carrying jade with you was thought to protect you from evil, and when held in the fist, it was believed that the virtues of the stone could be absorbed into the body. Narrow slivers of jade, in the form of wind chimes, were struck to attract a partner, and the sound they made was said to be the voice of the future admirer. By the middle of the nineteenth century, jade had become treasured as the essence of love itself.

In South East Asia, pearl divers in Borneo placed every ninth pearl they found in a bottle with two grains of rice per pearl, believing the pearl would magically reproduce itself – but only if the bottle-stopper was a dead man's finger! In Burma (now Myanmar) folk superstitions were attached to all kinds of everyday stones and rocks. People gathered wild rocks and pebbles, then placed them in their homes and worshipped them in the belief that the stones were inhabited by spirits, both good and bad. Blood offerings were then made to the stones to keep the spirits happy – if you didn't do this, the stone spirits would drain your blood instead.

The Americas

Pyrites (also known as fool's gold) was highly revered by North American indigenous peoples and was used for casting spells; to worship the ancestors or the Great Spirit (a mysterious creator god); and in healing rituals and vision quests (a rite of passage where male warriors sought out their personal spirit guide by journeying into the wilderness). The Maya people of Mesoamerica used pyrites to make scrying mirrors, which were used to divine the future: one side would be polished and flat for gazing into; the other would be convex and carved with mysterious symbols that summoned the spirits to reveal oracles. The Aztecs, however, preferred to use fine black obsidian for their scrying, as its surface and structure was perfect for making sheer, polished mirrors. They also used the stone to make sharp war daggers. Obsidian was known as *iztli* or *t'eotetl*, meaning 'divine stone', and was carved into totems of the god Tezcatlipoca, whose name means 'smoking mirror'. The god was believed to see all that occurred in the universe through the black stone.

The Incas used knives made from jade to tear out the

hearts of human sacrifices, which they then offered up to the rain god, while turquoise was the sacred stone of the Pueblo and Zuni Native American peoples. To the Apache, turquoise was known as *duklij*. Both green and blue varieties were highly prized for their talismanic influence. Unless he possessed a sacred turquoise, no shaman was considered worthy of his honourable status for healing and magic.

Now that we've explored some of the myths and stories that surround our beautiful friends, let's turn to some practical work to help you learn how to choose, care for and connect with your own crystals. With simple rituals and practices, you will discover how to create a crystal sanctuary; how to dedicate and programme crystals to align them to your personal needs and desires; and how to get prepared to work with their magic.

Chapter 2

Getting to Know Crystals and Sacred Stones

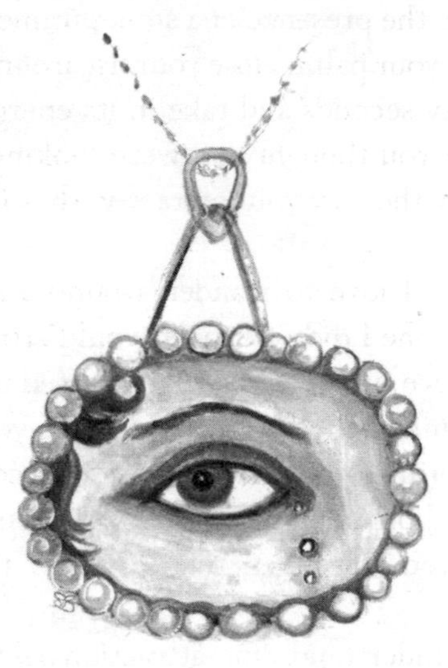

Choosing stones

A vast array of crystals and stones is currently available, ranging from prized pieces of rare tanzanite and black opal, to simple but highly effective clear quartz. Most of the stones suggested in this book are affordable and adorable.

Remember, your stones are your pals. They are alive with their own magical energy and ready to help you manifest your desires to allow you to take control of your life.

Shopping

When you go shopping for crystals, don't just choose the one that looks prettiest or sparkles best; choose the one that seems to be 'communicating' with you. If you see, hear or sense the presence of a stone, immediately pick it up, hold it in your palm, close your fist around it for maybe ten to twenty seconds and take in its energy. It may not be the stone you thought you were looking for, but you will know by the way you interact with it if it's the right one for you.

Personally, I love to wander around and find myself drawn to a stone I didn't expect would attract my attention. Stones are, it seems, just as attracted to us as we are to them. Think about what it's like when you meet a new friend. Sometimes you just feel an instant connection and immediately bond. It's the same with stones: often, it's the unexpected encounters that can prove to be the most fulfilling!

We can understand this attraction factor as a kind of universal resonance. The energies that flow between you and the stone generate a sense of familiarity, as if, somehow, you *know* this stone. The crystal's qualities are ones that you carry deep within you, too, and in that first moment of meeting, you may feel at home or at one with it because of that resonance.

Before you set off shopping, whether physically or on

the internet, perform this little ritual to open your mind and find clarity so that you can connect with the magical stones.

Visualisation Ritual for Choosing a Crystal

1. Find a relaxing spot. Close your eyes and focus for a few minutes on the kind of stones you are seeking.
2. Ask yourself:
    - Is the crystal you are seeking polished, rough, bright, sparkly, dull, dark or iridescent?
    - Do you have a certain type of crystal in mind, or are you open to anything?
    - Are there particular magical properties that you are looking for from your stone?
3. Visualise how the crystal will look in your home. Think about where will you keep it: do you have a dedicated space in mind just for that crystal, or will it be part of a grid arrangement that you want to create for home protection?
4. Imagine being faced with three different crystals: which one will you choose, and why? Will your choice be based on intuition or how the crystal looks? If, in this visualisation, you feel you have

made an intuitive choice, then you're on to the right track to choosing crystals that resonate with your energy. In their own way, they are choosing you, too.

5. Now imagine picking up one of the crystals and holding it in your hand. What would you like to feel: warmth, a spiritual connection, a flash of insight or realisation?
6. Open your eyes and thank the universe for helping you to engage with crystals. Now you are ready to choose a crystal and open yourself up to its magic.

Buying crystals online

If you're buying online, make sure you take the time to get to know your crystal. Once it arrives, hold it in your palm for a few minutes – if you don't get that immediate feeling of mutual empathy, remember that all stones will become your friends if you open your heart and soul to them. If you accept a stone into your life, you're accepting the magic of the universe.

These stones are saying something to you; they are living stones and their essence resonates with your current state of being. This is a sign that you're in tune with the energy of the crystal and its connection to universal power. So once the crystal is in your possession, repeat the following: 'My crystal friend, thank you for finding me.' Then perform the cleansing or programming rituals as needed (see pages 28 and 37).

Wild and wayside stones

As well as buying stones, whether in person or online, you may also come across 'wild' stones out in the natural world. This is where chance or meaningful coincidence, known as 'synchronicity', may be more important than rummaging around a shop. We'll explore wild stones and synchronicity in more detail on pages 39–42.

Crystal shapes and sizes

Crystals come in many shapes and forms, so I have outlined the most common types that you can buy online or in shops these days. It is important to bear in mind, however, that some crystals are created artificially to ensure a beautiful structure, so not everything that you see will have formed naturally.

For example, you'll often find tiny air bubbles in artificial clear quartz crystals, which you wouldn't see in natural stones. If you find that the colouring and shading of your crystal is inconsistent, it's a sign that it's the real deal. Manufactured stones are more likely to be uniform in colour, as they're often dyed. The best way to make sure you use authentic crystals is to go to a trusted and respected retailer.

Although rough, natural and terminated shapes are the most popular, palm or flat stones are great to carry with you when you're on the go. Ultimately, it all comes down to personal preference, so choose the stones that are going to be the most useful to you, and try to reflect on why you are attracted to a particular shape in the first place.

Natural

Most crystals are just little offcuts of rock left in its natural state. Some are polished, to create what are known as 'tumbled' stones. These natural-looking stones reveal the true matrix of the crystal's formation, and that's perhaps what makes them so attractive. You can carry these smaller stones with you, or you can place them in grids or in specific parts of the home to activate your intentions.

Terminated

Terminated crystals have pointed ends and are powerful tools for amplifying grid arrangements and intentions. Single-terminated crystals can remove negative energy or attract power, depending on where they are positioned. When pointed towards you, they attract power; when pointed away from you, they banish negativity. With double-terminated crystals, you can achieve these two effects simultaneously.

Geode

Useful for attracting abundance and success, geodes are usually small, cavern-like formations of rock lined with crystals. They can be placed anywhere in the home to enhance and empower the space, or can be positioned on your altar or sacred place to stimulate all practice work.

Cluster

These are usually clusters of ridges and points that stem out in different directions from a central base. They beam energy all over the surrounding area and are great to place in the home to enhance harmony and peace.

Phantom

A phantom is usually formed from many layers of quartz. Most commonly pyramid-shaped, phantom crystals are generally used for spiritual and healing work. In the home, they may be used for meditation and other spiritual work, and are particularly useful to help clarify what your deepest self truly seeks.

Ball

Famous for their use by clairvoyants, crystal balls are artificially formed spheres that radiate power. When you gaze into a crystal ball, it will reflect your current true desires. They are mostly used as an oracular tool for scrying and other forms of divination.

Flat or palm

These resemble the flat stones you may find on a beach, and can be held comfortably in the palm of one hand. They will help you focus on an intended goal and allow you to realise your desires.

Sceptre

Similar in shape to a magician's wand, sceptre-shaped stones will usually have a central rod with a larger portion of the crystal extending around it at one end. This shape is often used to reclaim power or to activate desire before you begin any rituals.

Caring for your crystals

Cleansing

Before you start using your crystals for magic work, it's important to understand how to look after them. If you care for your crystals, they will reward you by caring for you in turn, helping to attract those things you are seeking in your life.

When you buy or collect crystals, it's important to cleanse them of any negative energy they may have picked up on their travels. The early twentieth-century US mineralogist George Kunz called precious stones, 'haunted jewel houses'. He said that, just as a building can be haunted by past occupants, so too can gems and crystals that have been worn or handled by other people.

So, crystals need to be cleared of all energy, so that your own magic can come alive rather than be influenced by the past. Geopathic stress, i.e. electromagnetic energy and other invisible energies of the Earth, can also negatively affect crystals, so it's important to remove all forms of stressful energy.

By conducting a cleansing ritual, you can remove this energy and connect to the crystal from the moment you place it on your table. Your cleansed crystals will quickly become your friends after thousands of years of silent reverie deep below the Earth's surface.

We'll begin with a basic gentle purifying ritual, followed by an alignment ritual to ensure the crystal is in harmony with your intentions and psyche.

Simple cleansing

1. Gently immerse the stone in a stream, lake, ocean or fresh spring (or in a bowl of spring water) and hold it submerged for about a minute. As you do so, affirm – in your mind or out loud – that all negativity will be washed away, and positive energy will permeate the crystal.
2. Leave the crystal on a window ledge for twenty-four hours to recharge and reaffirm its positive qualities with solar and lunar power.

Four astrological elements alignment ritual

The energy of the four astrological elements (Fire, Earth, Air and Water) aligns the crystal with the planetary powers attributed to it and also to your own astrological make-up. This means you can work closely with your crystal knowing it is in harmony with your individual world.

You will need:

a crystal or crystals
a lit white candle (Fire)
a bowl of spring water (Water)
an acorn, oak leaf or image of either (Earth)
a mirror (Air)

1. Take your crystal and place it beside the lit candle: if you're working with multiple crystals, use them to form a circle around the candle to seal your intention.
   As you do so, say:

   'With Fire, I cleanse,
   align and bless you, my friend(s).'

2. Next, place the crystal or crystals in the bowl of water and leave to soak for a few minutes while you focus on the energy emanating from the water. Say:

   'With Water, I cleanse,
   align and bless you, my friend(s).'

3. Then place the crystal beside the oak leaf or acorn: if you're working with multiple crystals, use them to form a circle around the leaf to seal your intention. Say:

   'With Earth, I cleanse,
   align and bless you, my friend(s).'

4. Finally, place your crystal or crystals in front of the mirror and gaze into it, so that you can see both the crystal(s) and your face in the reflection. Say:

   'With Air, I cleanse, align and bless you, my friend(s).'

5. Thank the crystals for being there for you, then blow out the candle. Your crystals are now ready to be dedicated (see below), or they can be 'programmed' so their energy is focused on a specific goal (see page 36).

Dedication ritual

Once you have cleansed and aligned your crystals, you need to dedicate them with the intention that only positive energy will flow through them, and that they are only going to be used for the good of all. This dedication will also focus all the goodness of the universe into the crystals.

You will need:

cleansed crystals
a piece of paper and a pen (optional)
lavender essential oil
a handful of dry or fresh basil leaves

1. Place your cleansed crystals on your altar or sacred space to form a circle, or, if you don't have enough stones to make a circle, draw a big circle on a piece of paper, then place your crystals in the centre.
2. Sit in front of your circle of crystals and relax for a moment. Focus on your intention to use the crystals for universal harmony and your personal desires.
3. Moving in a clockwise direction, gradually sprinkle the basil leaves over the crystals, then drizzle a few drops of lavender oil across the basil to seal your intention.

   As you do so, repeat the following:

   'By light and truth will this ritual bring joy to all these crystals, so that they may in turn bring good energy to me and all who listen to the warm soul of the universe.'

4. Leave the circle of crystals overnight. In the morning, remove the basil. Your crystals will have received your dedication.

Connecting to the crystals

Finally, you need to show your trust in the crystals by honouring their elemental qualities or virtues, which correspond to their colour.

Earth

1. Earth stones are mostly green or brown, such as malachite, emerald, green aventurine or smoky quartz. Take your stone and bury it at the foot of a tree, under a bush or in a plant pot. As you do so, repeat the following charm:

   'With Earth I've blessed you, crystal dear
   To show my trust in you it's clear.'

2. Now leave in place overnight to allow the stone to be charged with Earth energy. When you go to remove the crystal the next day, be sure to repeat the charm again.

Air

1. Air stones are usually yellow or iridescent, such as citrine, amber and opal. On a windy day, leave your stone outside somewhere safe, but still exposed to the weather. Repeat the following charm as you do so:

   'With breath of wind you will be charmed
   And trust in me keeps you from harm.'

2. Return after twenty-four hours to collect the stone, repeating the charm as you do so. If you've been blessed with clear blue skies and no wind,

then blow directly on to the stone three times as if it were a dandelion seed head, symbolically invoking the energy of a breeze.

Fire

1. Fire stones are usually red, such as carnelian, tiger's rye or ruby. Leave your stone in direct sunlight for one day. As you position it, repeat the following charm:

   'With this flame I will be true
   To know you best and live for you.'

2. When you return the next day, kiss the crystal to seal your intention to work with its powers.

Water

1. For blue, clear and white crystals, such as moonstone, selenite or aquamarine, leave the stone outside in the rain for one night. If there's no rain, pour natural spring water over the stone and leave it in your chosen sacred spot.
2. As you do so, say:

   'This stone sees all belief in me
   To keep us close as close can be.'

3. When you return the next day, hold the stone to your forehead to connect its energy to your intuition.

Storing

Once you have a collection of crystals, you need to decide where to keep them. There are lots of different options: you can wrap them in silk scarves, place them in a special pouch, leave them in specific energising spots at home, or position them in a place that is sacred to you. Leaving them to gather dust is not an option: the stones won't thank you for it, and will only repay you with dusty energy!

My preference is to never shut them away in the dark. They are organic, of this Earth, and although they may come from the underground darkness and its extremes of temperature, they are now inspirited with their life above ground. They are here to lighten your way, so you should lighten theirs too.

To keep them vitalised with positive solar and lunar energy, create a crystal sanctuary where you can see, touch and hold them daily.

Creating a crystal sanctuary

If you are lucky enough to have some outside space – a garden, a terrace or even a balcony will do – then creating a little sanctuary outdoors will mean your crystals are well exposed to the natural powers of the sun, moon and planets. Of course, you might prefer to keep your stones indoors so that they are close at hand when you choose to practise spell work. Whatever your preference, you can transform your chosen spot into a sacred sanctuary by performing a short ritual to ensure positive and empowering energy.

Empowering and Protecting Ritual for Your Sanctuary

You will need:

a large, shallow glass bowl
4 white candles (to represent the four astrological elements)
dried rose petals

1. When you have decided on the location for your sanctuary, place the rose petals in the bowl and put it in the centre of your chosen spot.
2. Light the four candles. Place one to the north of the bowl, one to the south, one to the east and one to thc wcst.
3. Now say:

'With candle north will crystals align
With candle south will crystals shine
With candle east, will crystals heal
With candle west, will crystals feel.

Now bless this place as crystals' home
And make it sacred to my stones.'

4. Leave the bowl of rose petals in place for twenty-four hours and the sanctuary will be empowered with beneficial and protective energy. Remove the bowl, and, if you're working indoors, cover the flat surface with a silk scarf to 'mark' the spot. If you're outdoors, form a ring of pebbles or create a shrine of potted plants or flowers around this sacred space.
5. From now on, your crystals will be empowered by the sacred sanctuary you created. You can remove them and use them in grids and divination rituals and so on, but when you return them to this place, they will be safe and revitalised.

Programming

Crystals can be programmed so that their energy is focused on a specific goal, meaning your intention will be reinforced by the crystal's power. For example, if you are looking for new romance, you would programme a rose quartz crystal with your romantic intention. Once a stone has been programmed, it will continually work with that desire until it is cleared or reprogrammed. Although one crystal can enhance various intentions, it is important not to use the wrong crystal either. For example, if you're hoping for career growth, selenite would be the wrong crystal to programme as it is better employed for spiritual healing. Instead, you should opt for a green crystal, such as green tourmaline for enterprise and determination, or citrine for success.

Programming Ritual

1. Sit quietly with the selected crystal in your hand and focus on your intention. Make sure it's something related to the stone's qualities. Keep repeating this desire or intention over and over, either aloud or in your head.
2. Look at the crystal, and hold it close to your chest or belly. Repeat the intention at least seven times (this corresponds to the seven chakras) so the crystal attracts your desire to it.
3. Wear the stone, carry it in your pocket or place it by your bed, and keep it with you for at least twenty-four hours. It can also be beneficial to hold the crystal and repeat your intention several times a day.
4. Keep your programmed crystals out of contact with others to avoid them being influenced by other energies you don't want to attract.

Chapter 3

Working with Wild Stones and Other Ingredients

By wild stones, I mean those pebbles, stones and bits of rock you happen across on walks and when you're out and about in the natural world. You may consciously go out and forage for wild stones to add to your collection, as the joy of doing so is part of engaging with the natural world and connecting more deeply to its magical power. Or you may come across a particular stone by pure chance – although maybe it's not such a coincidence after all? Perhaps you were always supposed to meet this stone.

Is it, in fact, a moment of synchronicity, a meaningful coincidence for you?

Stones and synchronicity

Synchronicity is the experience of meaningful coincidences that are perhaps not so coincidental after all. But is it fate, or is it a sign of something greater at work?

Have you ever thought about someone, and then received a call from them the next minute? Have you ever had a dream, and encountered an element of that dream the next day? According to the influential psychologist Carl Jung, 'Synchronicity is an ever-present reality for those who have eyes to see.' Most people experience this through dreams, symbols, signs, numbers, 'random' events (such as choosing a tarot card or picking out a crystal for the day), conversations and spontaneous encounters. I believe there is meaning to be found in these signs and symbols, whether that's seeing a flock of birds flying above, or even dropping a piece of toast buttered side down. If a beautiful pebble washes up on the shore for me to find, this is a symbolic voice to which I listen.

Whether they are chance happenings or intentions woven by the universe, moments such as these can be hugely meaningful to us. The stones or crystals that we find, whether purely by chance or as a result of some deeper intention, will enable us to work in the symbolic world of magic with greater understanding.

Finding stones or learning to see them in a new way will not only benefit your magic work, it will also help to open you up to what does give you meaning in life, and therefore what your true desires are.

Here's how to welcome synchronicity in your magic work, and 'see' life from a more symbolic and meaningful viewpoint.

The wild stone ritual

1. The next time you go for a walk, look out for stones, rocks or pebbles. Does one of them catch your eye? Pick it up. Perhaps the stone is calling out to you in some way to embrace its ancient powers. Perhaps it carries an intrinsic energy that is reflected in your life right now. Don't overthink it. If it feels right, graciously take the stone.
2. On your way home, reflect on what attracted you to the stone. Hold it in your hand. Even if it's grubby, it doesn't matter. You are going to clean it of all negativity, as you did all your other crystals.
3. Before cleansing the stone, ask yourself these questions:

   - How do you resonate with this stone?
   - Does it make you feel warm, calm, excited, motivated, spiritual or energised?
   - Is it sharp, rough, round, flat, smooth, jagged or oval?

Try and describe its qualities out loud, then write them down.

4. Speak to the stone: look at it, tell it you care and explain that you want to befriend it.
5. Perform the simple cleansing ritual (page 28), then place it in your sacred place or sanctuary. It can be set apart from the other crystals if you like, and you can make a new separate collection of wild stones you discover at any time in the future.

How to work with wild stones

All wild stones can be used for both self-empowerment and serenity. Whether you opt to boost your self-confidence using the fine white quartz crystal you purchased or the tiny white stone you found by chance is up to you. In fact, you can use both the quartz and the wild stone in tandem, as self-empowerment comes from having a sense of serenity, and a sense of serenity comes from being self-empowered.

While other crystals and gemstones resonate to different colour vibrations that distinguish their usage, as you will see in the following chapters, wild stones don't generally comc in bright, vivid colours. You'll find that most arc shadcs of grey, white, black and brown. So, to help you decide the purpose your wild stones have for you, you will need to connect with how they make you feel.

Once you've cleansed your wild stones, take each one

in your hand and hold it in your fist for at least thirty seconds. How does it make you feel to hold it? Your reaction will tell you what purpose this stone has in your life. For example, if the stone makes you feel excited, warm or motivated, then you know it's a useful stone to use in self-empowerment rituals. If the stone is calming, then you know its use will lie in serenity magic.

Although your connection to each stone is more important than its colouring, if you're a beginner, you will probably find that working with crystals, where you can use their colour correspondences to identify their outstanding qualities, is the easiest way to get to know your own inner landscape before you work solely with wild stones.

Other ingredients used with crystal magic

Throughout this book, crystals are often combined with other ingredients in magic work to boost their influence or energise their power. These ingredients have symbolic associations with the crystals, because of either their colour or their elemental values. They are known as correspondences.

For example, a red carnelian's power is amplified by using red candles or certain red flowers. It can also be boosted by symbols and herbs associated with the element of Fire, such as ginger, or essential oils that incite passion, such as cedarwood. You might combine these with verses and incantations that invoke the sense of Fire.

On pages 265–271, you will find a glossary of ingredients you can use by correspondence as alternatives to the ingredients recommended. If you don't have one of the ingredients listed for a particular ritual in the book, just turn to the glossary to find an alternative.

Lunar and solar cycles

When working with these rituals, you will discover many of them require you to do so at a certain stage of the lunar cycle, as the energy of the moon at different stages can enhance and reinforce your magic work.

For magic purposes, this cycle begins with the new crescent moon, followed by the waxing moon, the full moon, the waning moon and the dark of the moon.

Throughout this book, you will find spells or rituals specifically aligned to these phases. Here's a brief rundown of how to use each phase of the moon for your own purposes.

New crescent moon

Perfect energy for spells and rituals concerned with fresh ideas, creative goals, new romance, fertility, new beginnings, communication, artistic inspiration and spiritual revival.

Waxing moon

The waxing moon will help you to perform spells to maximise any creative inclinations, put thoughts into action, develop or promote your goals, make it clear where you're going in a new relationship, and be open about your needs and desires.

Full moon

The full moon is a time for culmination: for finishing something that you've started, finalising a project, committing to a relationship or business deal, tying up loose ends, or confirming a future goal.

Waning moon

The waning moon is a time for letting go of the past and banishing negative thoughts. It is also the perfect time to give up bad habits or to try to kick an addiction.

Dark of the moon

The dark of the moon phase is when we're unable to see the moon. During this period, you can perform spells to enhance your meditation practice, reinforce emotional healing, understand your sacred self, or develop a deeper spiritual connection.

Now it's time to start working some magic in your life!

PART TWO
Collecting Crystals

It's always fun to create a crystal collection, but most of us start off with little knowledge and too much choice! This section tells you how to build your collection with five essential crystals, and those traditionally associated with the planets and the zodiac signs in astrology. Understanding the myths and magical uses associated with each crystal will help you to understand and harness its power. There's also a short section on collecting crystals depending on their colour and its resonance to specific qualities you may be looking to enhance or attract in life.

Chapter 4

Sacred Stone Collection

When you first start collecting stones for magical work, it's sensible to have a general balance of colour, meaning, symbolic association and magical power to get you started.

Colour correspondence

The colour of crystals is hugely important because every colour resonates to certain qualities and energies in our lives. For example, blue will allow you to enhance your spiritual or psychic connection, while red correlates to passion, green to manifestation, yellow to communication, and so on. A collection of only red stones would certainly invoke passion and invite action and adventure in to your life, but you would be less connected to your sense of universal meaning and inner magic (clear quartz crystals), or intuition (blue and purple stones). So balancing the colours in your collection and including one of each of the five major colours, which correspond to the five magical elements, will promote beneficial results and sacred integration.

The magical elements

The five magical elements are: Earth, Air, Fire, Water and Spirit.

In Western magic, four of these elements (the astrological elements) correspond to the compass points and also the four directions used in Wicca. Earth corresponds to north, Fire to south, Air to east and Water to west. The fifth element, often known as the quintessential element, quintessence or spirit, unifies them all. In Western magic, you are the spirit who stirs into life the energy of your crystals.

Earth colours: dark greens, browns and black
Air colours: soft greens, yellows, opaline and multi-coloured
Fire colours: reds and dark oranges
Water colours: blues and purples
Spirit colours: clear

The five elemental crystals

By working with the Western magic tradition of the five elemental crystals, you will have an immediate universal connection. Even if you don't collect all the other crystals mentioned in this chapter, these five are essential for casting spells and performing rituals.

Spirit crystal: clear quartz
Earth crystal: malachite
Air crystal: opal
Fire crystal: fire agate
Water crystal: kyanite

The Spirit crystal: clear quartz

Preferably, your Spirit crystal should be a double-terminated clear quartz crystal wand (see page 25), but if you find it hard to get hold of one of these, then any shape of clear quartz crystal will be able work its magic until you can acquire a more potent wand. You could also use phantom quartz, which has inclusions of smaller crystals in the main crystal to create ghostly shapes, or clear rutilated quartz, which has pretty needle-like inclusions of rutile (a deep burgundy and brown mineral composed of titanium oxide).

Magical attributes

Helps with focus, positive energy, manifesting intentions and revealing truth.

Healing

Offers clarity of mind, calms the body, restores balance and promotes spiritual healing.

Chakra

All chakras.

Mystery and magic

Clear quartz crystal has long been associated with divination and prophecy, and was believed by different ancient civilisations to be sent from the gods, or, as the ancient Sumerians believed, to have fallen to Earth from outer worlds or icy realms in the sky. Gazing into a crystal, sibyls of Apollo's temples would divine the future by reading the patterns and decoding the images they saw inside the stone. Ancient Greek seers would breathe on to the crystal (as if to mist up the facets), then quickly polish the mist away with their hair. If any part of the crystal remained misty, the shapes and patterns would be interpreted. If all the mist cleared, it was a sign that beneficial influences would come to the seeker.

Use

In healing and magical work, clear quartz crystals are used to attract rewards and success, and activate results. They are often used as reinforcements in crystal grids (see page 171) to empower any ritual or spell with vitalising energy. In divination, clear quartz signifies active, positive results, the truth and power of knowledge, enlightened thinking and deeper wisdom.

The Earth crystal: malachite

Magical attributes

Helps with protection, grounding, manifesting, finding oneself, attracting wealth and success.

Healing

Clears emotional imbalance, and restores stamina, self-belief and stability.

Associated chakra

Heart.

Mystery and magic

Mystical associations connect this beautiful green stone with the heart of the forest and the magic of ancient dryad rituals. These woodland glades were also where medieval sorcerers would perform rites to find their true connection to the magic of nature by intentionally getting lost in the depths of the forest. If carried, malachite was prized for its ability to help you find your way again if you ever got lost. In Classical times, the stone was carved with symbols such as the sun or sigils of the various planetary energies to attract luck or wealth, and was worn as a pendant or carried in a purse to protect from the Evil Eye.

Use

Placed in the home, malachite brings stability and security to whoever lives there, as well as attracting positive energy and even abundance, particularly if placed in the south-eastern corner of the home (according to the principles of feng shui). In a divination reading, malachite can indicate emotional truth is needed, or that it's time to move on and forgive or let go of the past. Malachite is used in magic rituals to free you from negative emotions and attract well-being, and in protective spells to counter blame, envy or negativity from others.

The Air crystal: opal

Magical attributes

Helps with transformation, progress, optimism, intuition, imagination, spontaneity and creativity.

Healing

Cures optical problems, boosts low self-esteem and frees one from inhibitions.

Associated chakra

Crown.

Mystery and magic

Once known as the 'eye stone' because it was believed by classical physicians to heal a multitude of eye complaints, opal's iridescence gives the stone a magical luminosity depending on the angle of light. The stone was believed by ancient Babylonian magicians to bestow the wearer with the gift of invisibility. The Romans thought the stone embodied all the other gemstones because of its many different colours, and during the medieval period it was worn to improve sight or bring good luck. Although it fell into disfavour in the nineteenth century thanks to its association with a curse on the heroine of Sir Walter Scott's popular novel, *Anne of Geierstein*, it's a crystal that strengthens the mind, brings the wearer a sense of purpose, optimism and self-worth, and attracts good luck in life.

Use

Opal is used as an empowering and revelatory stone for spells and rituals when you need to discover your way forward, reach a goal, reflect, use logic and clear your mind of toxic emotions. With its multi-coloured, dazzling array of rainbow lights and inspirational energy, opal amplifies any desire for adaptability and change when used in grids and ritual work. Its appearance in a divination reading reveals success and new opportunities.

The Fire crystal: fire agate

Magical attributes

Enhances true desires, passion, charisma and sexuality; attracts fame.

Healing

Aids digestive disorders, promotes self-protection, increases sexual vitality, and clears writer's block.

Associated chakra
Sacral.

Mystery and magic
A variegated form of chalcedony, fire agate shimmers with iridescent flashes of orange, red and gold showing off its fiery qualities. Ancient Greek and Roman magi used the stone to protect against danger, cure serpent bites and attempt to control the weather or divert storms. Believing this particular agate to contain the essence of pure fire, medieval alchemists used the stone in their quest to turn lead into gold. They placed several stones beneath their alembic (a distilling container) to reinforce the alchemical process known as calcination, a form of purification. By heating the lead to an extremely high temperature, any volatile substances were removed, and the metal purified before the next stage of the process.

Use
To accelerate and enhance any new plans or projects, and to achieve results, simply place fire agate in a south-facing windowsill. Fire agate used in magic rituals or spells enhances creativity, removes blockages, opens your mind and gives you the motivation and passion to get ahead. It enhances courage, and in grid work can create a powerful shielding force around you, bringing you the opportunities you truly wish for. In a divination reading, fire agate implies a fantastic chance is coming your way or that it is the time for action.

The Water crystal: kyanite

Magical attributes

Offers psychic power, a release from illusions, the ability to see the truth, connection to inner magic, and the ability to transmit and receive love.

Healing

Aids adrenal glands and the thyroid, deepens insight, and heals emotional wounds.

Associated chakras

Throat and heart.

Mystery and magic

This stone derives its name from the Greek, *kyanos*, meaning 'deep blue'. Although sometimes a mix of soft blues, stratified with pinks and greys, kyanite, when polished, was often mistaken for the rarer gemstone blue sapphire, before its geological structure was analysed and formally identified in the eighteenth century. One story from the Italian Renaissance describes how a lady was given a prized gemstone necklace made of fine rubies and sapphires by her much older goldsmith husband-to-be. Delighting in a secret liaison with a younger admirer, the necklace snapped. She managed to find all of the stones, except for one blue sapphire. Not wanting her future husband to know, she replaced it with a blue sapphire from a ring that he had also given her. One night, gazing lovingly into the lady's eyes (or at the gemstones), the goldsmith saw scratches on the blue sapphire. Knowing it was impossible to scratch a sapphire, he realised the stone had been replaced. In fact, the ring he had crafted for her had been made with kyanite, which he described as a rare blue sapphire, so he realised this was the same stone. Perhaps they were well matched in their deceit after all?

USE

The perfect stone to enhance all forms of loving relationships and to bring you closer to your emotional needs when used in spells and rituals. Placed in your home, it creates loving energy, and enables you to understand others, accept their faults and see the truth of who you are. As part of a larger grid, kyanite infuses intuitive and psychic power into your magical process, and gives you access to the power of the universe. In divination readings, kyanite signifies that illusions can be cast aside, and that you are in control of your destiny.

The three power stones

When you perform any of the rituals or divination readings in this book, place these three power stones in a triangle close by: the first to boost or amplify energy, the second to protect you from unwanted forces, and the third to energise your connection to the power of natural magic.

Guide stone

For amplifying the energy of spells, grids and practices. Choose clear quartz crystals or rainbow quartz to enhance all forms of illumination, both spiritually and psychologically.

Protection stone

To protect you from negativity and psychic or geopathic stress. Chose a black or dark brown stone, such as onyx, black tourmaline or smoky quartz.

Focus stone

A sacred, personal stone for universal magic power. This is your private, sacred stone, often kept in a place separate from your other crystals. As your bestie stone, it can be any stone of your choice, in any colour, shape or size you prefer.

THREE STONE PREPARATION RITUAL

You will need:

guide stone
focus stone
protection stone
a white candle
a handful of dried lavender flowers or sprigs
of lavender

1. Place the three stones so they form a triangle, with the focus stone at the top, the guide stone at the bottom left, and the protection stone at the bottom right.
2. Place the candle in the middle of the triangle and light it.
3. Hold the lavender while you repeat the following incantation, gazing into the candle flame to find stillness with your crystals:

'My focus stone to bring me power
Is blessed and ready for me now,
Protection stone, oh keep me safe
From all that can't be seen with faith,
And last my guide stone, true and fair,
Will bring me to the magic air.'

4. Slowly sprinkle the lavender around the triangle in a clockwise direction and repeat the incantation. Close your eyes for ten seconds and find stillness. Open your eyes, blow out the candle and gather your crystals. They are now ready to aid you in your spell work or rituals, to vitalise your own magic powers.

The ten planet crystals

Traditionally, the use of crystals in magic is associated with the planets and their symbolism. Thousands of years ago, these planetary qualities were believed to be embodied in each crystal. Many civilisations, such as the ancient Greeks, Babylonians and Romans, believed planets to be deities. As the system of astrology developed, the constellations, and more precisely, the zodiac, were assigned planetary rulers.

I have compiled the following list of planet crystals based on the traditional magical powers attributed to each stone and its correspondence to each sign or planet. These crystals will boost your magical connection to each planet's qualities.

If you do manage to collect them all, you will have a perfect balance of energy, but don't feel that you need a complete collection immediately: you can build up your collection as you go, acquiring the stones as and when you can.

THE TEN PLANET CRYSTALS

The following crystals will boost your magical connection to each planet's qualities which the ancient Babylonian astrologers believed to be embodied in specific stones.

The sun: sunstone

Solar light and the sun's energy are at the root of our existence, and the sun amplifies the magic of personal power, individuality and our sense of purpose or meaning in life.

Keywords

Joy, success, initiative, confidence, inner strength, willpower.

Healing use

Restores self-belief, nurtures spirit, aids metabolism and enhances life-force and vitality.

Chakras

Base and sacral.

Mystery and myth

Sparkling like the sun, the inclusions of goethite or hematite refract light between the crystal's layers and produce an iridescent effect when viewed from various angles. The ancient Babylonian magi believed the stone was part of the sun itself and used it as a centrepiece in magic rituals to propitiate the sun god and receive beneficial solar energy and the god's blessing. Medieval witches would lay a grid of sunstones around them on a full moon night to receive the positive energy of the sun's light shining on the moon. In Hindu folklore, a sunstone held out to the full moon was believed to bring luck for the rest of the month.

Magic use

Sunstone is a vitalising stone amplifying initiative and courage. It can be used in spells to attract abundance, success and good fortune. In grids, it protects you from your own inner demons and empowers you with self-awareness and the strength to communicate the truth.

When it appears in a divination reading, sunstone indicates progress, fresh ideas and a chance to prove yourself. Placed in the south corner of your home, sunstone enhances all forms of career opportunities and successful work projects.

The moon: selenite

In astrology, the moon governs our feelings, intuition, moods and sense of security, and reveals to us our true needs. This ever-changing lunar cycle corresponds to our instinctive, ephemeral nature, and reminds us to go with the flow.

Keywords

Clarity, serenity, intuition, contentment, security, fertility, trusting one's instincts, knowing one's inner self.

Healing use

Calms, clears emotional blockages, clears negative energy fields, and enhances spiritual connection.

Chakra

Third eye.

Mystery and myth

Its luminous, translucent glow gives this stone a mysterious aura. Named after the Greek moon goddess, Selene, who drives her silver chariot across the sky, selenite's delicate structure is subtle and varied, yet belies an inner radiance. Associated with Selene's power to hypnotise the mortal Endymion, to whom she made love every night, the stone was used in medieval love magic to seduce and hypnotise the object of one's desire. The sibyls of ancient Greece used selenite for scrying and crystal gazing, with its strange structure often revealing ghostly images depending on the light of the moon.

Magic use

Selenite can be used in spells cast for enlightenment or new understanding, to achieve a serene lifestyle or to bring clarity to a situation. In love, it is a great enhancer of harmony, romance and fidelity, while placing it in the home will bring protection and security. When it appears in a divinatory reading, the stone signifies reconciliation or positive negotiations are on the horizon. Use selenite wands in grids to amplify your spiritual connection to the universe, or to add lunar power to other crystals in the grid.

Mercury: sodalite

Well known for its association with all forms of communication, Mercury enables us to transmit ideas and trade thoughts, reflect, inspire others or simply adapt to the many changes we all experience in life.

Keywords

Transition, diversity, fun, communication, telepathy, flexibility, understanding, clarity of mind.

Healing use

Aids the immune system, helps with meditation, and helps with peaceful negotiations.

Chakras

Throat, brow.

Mystery and myth

Sometimes confused with lapis lazuli, although it lacks its gold specks, this lovely blue stone was first discovered in nineteenth-century Greenland. It soon became a popular decorative stone used in stately European interiors, particularly in marble inlay flooring and mosaic work. Known as the poet's stone or writer's stone, one apocryphal nineteenth-century tale tells of the author of an occult work, who, after several months of writer's block, was given a piece of sodalite. He placed the stone on his writing bureau and within three weeks he had completed his book.

Magic use

To bring logic, focus and clear communication to all negotiations, the stone can be carried with you, or it can be placed in the home to bring wit, insight, negotiation and vivacity to any social event. In grids, it keeps the mind balanced between logic and intuition, and in divination it signifies the need to express yourself, or to listen carefully and read between the lines. To enhance the power of the mind, sodalite can be used in spell work. It also boosts all forms of focused writing, reading or creative work.

Venus: rose quartz

Renowned as the planet of love, Venus also reminds us of our sense of vanity and self-worth, and asks us to consider our relationships – not only with others, but with nature, too. Venus influences our values and our sense of beauty, and asks us how fair are we in love and war?

Keywords

Unconditional love, healing, self-worth, value, beauty, grace.

Healing use

Helps with emotional healing, works as an aphrodisiac, promotes personal fulfilment and aids the reproductive system.

Chakras

Heart and base.

Mystery and myth

A famous Greek myth describes how Aphrodite, the goddess of love, fell head over heels for Adonis, a mortal. Aphrodite was so enthralled with her young Adonis that their relationship drew the ire and jealousy of her former lover Ares, the god of war. Fuelled by rage and resentment, Ares adopted the form of a wild boar and attacked Adonis. In Aphrodite's haste to save her mortal lover, she grazed her arm on a briar bush as she rushed down from Olympus. Holding a mortally wounded Adonis in her arms, Aphrodite's blood mingled with that of her lover, and legend has it that this is how rose quartz was formed.

Gazing into a rose quartz crystal, medieval scryers were able to 'see' the future husband of a maiden, or even the number of children she would bear. Prized for enhancing romance spells, and used in all forms of love magic, rose quartz is renowned for being the ultimate emotional healer and for attracting one's heart's desire.

Magic use

Rose quartz is used in spells to attract new love, romance or a better understanding of others. When combined with herbs, roses and other natural magic ingredients, the crystal fulfils all desires and enhances our ability to love others as well as ourselves. When placed in the home, the crystal amplifies sensuality, while a grid made up entirely of rose quartz can be created to ensure a successful love match. In divination, rose quartz indicates that love is in the air – or that you need to evaluate your feelings for someone.

Mars: bloodstone

The planet of motivation and action, Mars encourages us to go about getting what we want, and shows us the best way to do it. Mars represents our ego, will and sex drive, as well as the challenges, risks or battles each of us must face in life.

Keywords

Action, motivation, will, strength, courage, decision-making, good luck in competitions.

Healing use

Aids eye and blood ailments, helps with detoxification and offers physical protection.

Chakra

Base.

Mystery and myth

Bloodstone, known as heliotrope in ancient Greece, has a long legacy of magical tales and uses. It was considered a stone of invisibility (as recorded by Roman historian Pliny), yet one could see the sun at its centre even during a solar eclipse. Carried by Roman soldiers, it was thought to protect the body and staunch the flow of blood in wounded men. A later Christian myth suggested that the red specks in the stone were created from the blood of Christ as it dripped from his wounds when he was nailed to the cross, which then fell on to green jasper rock below. Ancient Mesopotamian priests used the stone in healing, dipping bloodstone into cold water that was then placed on the patient's body to transfer the life-giving force of the sun, or to prevent injury or disease.

Magic use

In spells and rituals, bloodstone is the ultimate stone to boost the ego, give courage and make you feel invincible. Carrying this stone means you can progress with any plans. In divination, its positive placement suggests it's time to achieve your ambitions, or a sign that you can defeat all obstacles in your path. If you're in a difficult position, it may be prudent to take a reality check and not be impulsive. Placing bloodstone in the home will reinforce a balance of energy, both motivating and balancing occupants while protecting them from outside negativity.

Saturn: smoky quartz

Stern Saturn embodies the qualities of determination, sagacity, stamina, purpose and ambition. The planet also describes our defences and boundaries, our sense of time and space, and what we can best achieve in our careers and lives.

Keywords

Enterprise, manifestation, ambition, determination, grounding, protection, discipline.

Healing use

Restores emotional strength, self-control and self-confidence, and banishes negativity and stress.

Chakras

Base, sacral.

Mystery and myth

The deep, dusky colours of smoky quartz were thought by the ancient magi to hold the secrets to the universe, and ancient Greek, Roman and Mesopotamian scryers favoured smoky quartz above clear quartz when searching for esoteric information. The crystal was also used in medieval Europe to protect against evil forces, and was sometimes carved into a cross and hung above the owner's bed. It was made into seals and rings, with charms, sigils or symbols engraved into the stone to protect the wearer from danger and to promote strength of purpose.

Magic use

In spell work, smoky quartz protects against negative energy, and grounds and connects you to the magic of the Earth itself. For rituals to boost career, improve your self-esteem or manifest specific intentions, the crystal enhances your resolve and is perfect for helping to culminate ambitions if used during a full moon. Placing smoky quartz in the home aids emotional strength, determined focus and protects from most negative energies. If used in divination, its placement usually suggests a time to knuckle down and overcome obstacles.

(By the way, smoky quartz is one of the most trafficked stones, so make sure you acquire it from a reputable source. False smoky quartz is dyed clear quartz and won't have the same grounding effect.)

Jupiter: lapis lazuli

Jupiter is associated with expansive energy, and gives opportunities and chances to those who seek them out. Jupiter embodies good luck, generosity, abundance and persuasive power, but most importantly, it teaches us that universal wisdom will get you places.

Keywords
Conviction, adventure, boundless ideas, truth, self-belief, clarity and wisdom.

Healing use
Aids the nervous system, helps with migraines, vertigo and throat problems, increases psychic powers.

Chakras
Throat and brow.

Mystery and myth
Renowned for its intense blue colour and flecks of gold (pyrites), lapis lazuli was ground down and used to create the intense and prized ultramarine pigment favoured by Renaissance artists. The magical, deep, cobalt blue of the stone was prized by the ancient Egyptians, who believed the gold flecks were embodiments of the gods in the night sky. Lapis lazuli was thus extensively used in jewellery, as well as to decorate tombs and burial chambers and in funerary adornment. It was also used to create magical elixirs. Egyptian royalty favoured the stone to such an extent that it was ground down into powder and used as eyeshadow. Later, Greek sorcerers used the stone in rituals to summon beneficial spirits, such as the protective genii of the home.

Magic use
Lapis is the perfect stone to include in any ritual or spell to attract success, good luck or self-acceptance. In grids, it

enhances personal motivation, and in divination it signifies chances coming your way or travel opportunities that will bring success. Placed in the entrance of your home, lapis will encourage good fortune and achievement.

Uranus: green aventurine

Not discovered until the mid-eighteenth century, Uranus is associated with the god of the heavens, Ouranos. Both the planet and the god embody openness, unconditional love, free-spirited attitudes and opportunist methods.

Keywords

Opportunity, change, radical thought, individuality, breaking through, unconditional love.

Healing use

Anti-inflammatory. It can calm anger, protect against stress and bring love.

Chakra

Heart.

Mystery and myth

The beautiful colour of this green stone was prized throughout the ancient world. It was used to decorate statues, figurines and monuments, as well as in ancient Greek mosaic work and Egyptian tombs. To attract opportunity in Celtic folk magic, the stone was buried beneath an oak tree on a full moon night, removed in the morning, and then placed in a jar of water and left for one lunar cycle.

In feng shui, it's believed to bring successful love affairs or great opportunities when placed in the western corner of your home. In Vedic mythology, green aventurine was thought to embody the powers of the love god, Vishnu, and to see two of the same stones together promised a forthcoming love union.

Magic use

Used in spells along with green herbs such as basil and sage, aventurine invites fresh starts, not forgetting breakthroughs and enlightenment in creative pursuits. In divination readings, the crystal indicates it's time to break free, or to accept that a change is coming in your life. When used in a grid around the home, aventurine is another stone that can be used to protect against geopathic stress in the environment. It can also be carried when travelling to protect the wearer from all forms of unwanted electromagnetic and other invisible energies.

Neptune: celestite

Neptune is the planet of dreams, imagination, surrender, release, idealism and the outer limits of the unconscious. Using Neptune's crystal will connect you to your spiritual self but also to higher realms of the universe.

Keywords

Release from reality, spiritual liberation, psychic power, creativity, compassion, intuition.

Healing use

Relieves stress, calms moods, aids deep meditation and cools emotions.

Chakras

Crown, third eye, throat.

Mystery and myth

This beautiful soft blue stone was first named at the end of the eighteenth century, and has few legends surrounding it. Another form of it is called celestine, both names referring to the celestial realm reflected in its heavenly soft blue colour. One celestite geode formation has become an important tourist attraction in a limestone cave on South Bass Island in Lake Erie, Ohio. In 1887, a man named Gustav Heineman emigrated from Germany to the island, where he established a winery. While digging a well, he discovered a cave filled with celestine crystals. He turned the property into a tourist attraction, meaning his winery was able to survive the Prohibition era. The cave's remarkable celestine crystals, some up to 1 metre (3 feet) wide, can still be viewed.

Magic use

In contemporary magic traditions, celestite is renowned for its ability to help connect you to the angelic realm, so you can access your guardian angel or call on archangels such as Gabriel and Michael. It is thought to be a beneficial stone when placed in the home for anyone involved in creative work, reviving inspiration and reinforcing artistic or literary talents. When it occurs in a reading, the stone in a positive position indicates creative abilities are about to be showcased; when in a blockage position, it reminds you to take care not to be led astray by your ideals or illusions.

Pluto: black tourmaline

Discovered in the twentieth century and infamous for its red snow and heart-shaped glacier, this icy dwarf planet describes where we unearth our inner treasure, or where we must dig deep to find our personal power. Beneficial Pluto energy allows us to transform hidden powers and use it in the external world.

Keywords

Defence, protection, defining boundaries, personal power, transformation.

Healing use

Removes geopathic stress and negative emotions, and aids the immune system.

Chakras

Base, sacral.

Mystery and myth

Also known as shorl, black tourmaline has been used by shamans, sorcerers and witches worldwide as a protective stone when casting spells and performing rituals. Its magnetic polarity (when the stone is heated or rubbed) was believed to ward off evil influences, and an apocryphal tale of Marie de Medici tells how she wore a ring made of a piece of tourmalated quartz (clear quartz crystal with fine needles of shorl embedded in the centre) to protect her from poisoners. Considered a stone of physical and emotional safety, indigenous Native American tribal nations such as the Cherokee carried black tourmaline to protect them from negative energy during vision quests, a rite of passage undertaken when an individual reached adulthood, which saw them sent out into the wilderness to engage with a spirit guide.

Magic use

In divination, black tourmaline indicates a time to reveal the truth or to dig deep into your soul to decide what has inner meaning for you. In magic spells and rituals, black tourmaline is a protective stone, but it can also reinforce any desire or intention to transform your life. As a power stone, it is often used in grids to amplify and protect the message or desire, and when placed in the home, it will protect you from all kinds of negativity.

Chapter 5

Zodiac Crystals

The zodiac is the imaginary belt surrounding the Earth according to the ecliptic (the apparent path of the sun). It is divided into twelve thirty-degree segments, which together make up the 360 degrees of a circle. There are many crystals and sacred stones assigned to each zodiac sign, and various traditions prefer some crystals to others. Here, I have chosen the crystals that are easiest to obtain and align most obviously with each zodiac sign's qualities based on Western magic traditions. If you have the time, opportunity and resources to add these twelve zodiac stones to your collection, you will have the complete magic crystal kit at your disposal!

Depending on your own sun sign, wearing or carrying your own zodiac stone will bring out your best qualities. If you prefer, you can choose it as your focus or personal stone to sit beside you whenever you perform magic.

Aries

Qualities: bold, daring, passionate, impulsive, courageous, self-important, action-taker

Carnelian (reddest shades best)

Keywords

Success, enterprise, determination, self-worth, direction.

Healing use

Balances energy flow, calms emotional stress and prevents envy.

Chakra

Sacral.

Mystery and myth

In ancient Egypt, red carnelian amulets were engraved with verses from the *Book of the Dead* and placed on a mummy's neck to ensure the soul had a safe journey to the afterlife. Carnelian was believed to be endowed with the power of Isis, the Egyptian goddess of magic, meaning the soul would be under her protection. In medieval Europe, carnelian amulets and rings were engraved with magical designs and symbols to protect the wearer. A thirteenth-century treatise describes how a carnelian engraved with a sword-bearing male figure would guard the wearer from vice and bewitchment, as well as protecting their surroundings from lightning, storms and tempests.

Magic use

Wearing carnelian gives you courage, passion and determination to succeed. In spells and rituals, it can incite romantic or physical desire, boost your ambitions or career pathway, and increase chances of prosperity. Using carnelian in grids around the home will prevent bad feelings among family members and help to nurture loving relationships. In divination reading, a positive placement of red carnelian indicates creative opportunity or future success coming your way; in a negative position, it suggests that you need to hold back your impulses and go with the flow.

Taurus

Qualities: determined, consistent, loyal, compassionate, reliable, practical, stubborn

Emerald

KEYWORDS
Abundance, wisdom, integrity, inner strength, loyalty in love, self-acceptance, honesty.

HEALING USE
Used for detoxification; also clears emotional negativity and aids eye complaints.

CHAKRAS
Heart, throat.

MYSTERY AND MYTH
Ancient Mesopotamian sorcerers believed every emerald embodied the essence of the goddess Ishtar, and used the stone in their rituals to ward off evil influences. In Vedic belief, the emerald in Vishnu's necklace was thought to symbolise the Earth as being the centre of all human passion. According to medieval grimoires, emeralds placed under the tongue bestowed prophetic powers, riches and quick wits. The Roman emperor Nero was said to have gazed at his reflection in a huge emerald that gave him the gift of prophecy. Ancient Persian tradition tells

of how the emerald should never be worn when making love, as it deflates sexual desire. However, by the Middle Ages, the emerald had become treasured for its ability to increase wealth, augment sensual pleasure, increase prestige and divert storms. In *Gargantua*, a nineteenth-century mythical novel by Rabelais, the hero giant's codpiece was fastened with a buckle set with two orange-sized emeralds to boost his erection! Medieval Christian lapidaries (books describing the virtues of precious and semi-precious stones) confirmed the emerald's ability to empower the wearer with faith, hope, loyalty, wisdom and harmony.

Magic use

With its generous qualities ranging from integrity to fidelity, self-belief and inner strength, the emerald is an essential stone in any collection. It can be used to improve memory, remove fear and clear away negative thinking. In grids, the emerald promotes abundance, good fortune and a richness of spirit and soul. When an emerald appears in a divination reading in a positive placement, it indicates determination will bring success; in a blockage placement, it suggests you need to work harder on your own self-belief to get results.

Gemini

Qualities: flexible, light-hearted, fun-loving, creative, enthusiastic, outgoing, imaginative, expressive, witty

Citrine

Keywords
Self-expression, happiness, success, abundance, imagination, fresh start.

Healing use
Clears negative thinking, and enhances stamina and intelligence.

Chakras
Solar plexus and sacral.

Mystery and myth
Citrine is a quartz ranging in colour from pale, fresh yellow to light orange. It isn't referred to by name in any myth, folklore or legend. It may have been mistaken for a form of topaz known as chrysolite, yellow sapphire or golden beryl, or identified solely as 'crystallus', which was the ancient name given to all forms of rock crystal. The easy availability of quartz means it was used worldwide by shamans, seers and magicians for anything from scrying mirrors to talismans and amulets engraved

with various figures to attract love, banish envy, reveal truth and promote commercial success. The true yellow variety, however, is found mostly in Brazil, Madagascar, Spain and Russia. It became popular in the nineteenth century, and enjoyed a later surge of popularity in the art deco period when it was used in designer pieces of jewellery.

Magic use

Inspires optimism and brings hope: this is a stone of abundant happiness if cared for in the home. In spells, it can be combined with other stones to boost their own qualities and to add motivation and dynamic action to all personal desires. When worn or carried as an amulet, citrine attracts good company, sparkling conversation, wit and social acceptance. In divination, it can indicate that it's time to open up discussions or explore creative ideas, but in a negative position, it signifies that being too flippant or frivolous could lead to difficult negotiations.

Cancer

Qualities: caring, intuitive, supportive, giving, imaginative, protective, sensitive, belonging

Moonstone

Keywords

Self-understanding, acceptance, protection, calm, sacred self.

Healing use

Aids menstrual problems and fertility, helps to maintain hormonal balance, and calms emotion.

Chakra

Crown.

Mystery and myth

As its name suggests, moonstone has long been associated with the lunar cycle. In medieval times, the stone was used in spells, particularly during a full moon, to enhance fertility or to restore lovers' passion. Made up predominantly of feldspars, rocks formed from mineral deposits, the stone displays an iridescence that symbolises the glow of the moon in its different phases. The sixteenth-century French physician and astronomer Antonio Mizauld wrote about how a moonstone owned by a travelling friend would indicate the waxing and waning of the moon due to a fine inclusion within the stone that moved to the middle of the stone during a full moon, and returned to the tip at a new moon. In fact, by gazing into a moonstone at both these phases, you'll discover for yourself some very different shapes and images you could use for divination purposes.

Magic use

Mostly used to promote imagination and inspiration, to enhance fertility and for protection, the moonstone is also the perfect stone for use in meditation and divination – and, of course, for working with the changing cycles of the moon. It can be used in grids and spells at certain phases to boost their specific energy. In divination, it indicates that it's time to listen to your intuition, or that now is the perfect moment for a new beginning or fresh start.

Leo

Qualities: individuality, vitality, ardour, self-confidence, big-heartedness, luxury-loving

Tiger's eye

Keywords

Success, confidence, self-motivation, lucky chances, willpower, clarity.

Healing use

Dispels fears and anxiety, aids decision-making, balances energy.

Chakras

Sacral, base and solar plexus.

Mystery and myth

Displaying luminescent bands of light known as 'chatoyancy', similar to those seen in its more expensive and iridescent relative cat's eye, tiger's eye has been used for thousands of years for its protective, reflective powers. The more inclusions of bands of light, the more powerful the stone. These moving lines are important symbols in divination. Ancient seers would cast tiger's eye into a circle and, depending on the way the lines of light moved, would determine the querent's future. In ancient Egypt, the stone was considered an all-seeing eye, giving the wearer the ability to see through walls, doors and beyond into the afterlife. By the medieval period, the stone was also used to see through people's motives and to see the truth of a loved one's fidelity.

Magic use

When worn as a pendant or a ring, tiger's eye boost self-confidence and promotes others' confidence in you and affection for you. In spells and rituals concerned with success, the addition of tiger's eye will lead to speedy results and a positive outcome. As a divination stone, in a positive placement it indicates good luck and opportunities coming your way. In a negative position, it's a sign to listen to advice and not leap in at the deep end.

Virgo

Qualities: discriminating, decisive, responsible, reliable, adaptable, analytical

Peridot

KEYWORDS
Self-reliance, clarity, awakening, focus, stress relief.

HEALING USE
Vitalises the metabolism and aids the respiratory system.

CHAKRAS
Heart and solar plexus.

MYSTERY AND MYTH
This beautiful light green stone (also known as chrysolite and, in its darker shade, olivine) is said to have been found on the mystical Serpent Island in the Red Sea. The stone (then known as a topaz) was highly prized by the ancient Egyptians, and legend tells of how the island was guarded by mythical 'watchers' to prevent anyone unauthorised from finding the stones. Those who were permitted access on behalf of the pharaohs would only be able to see the radiant stones after nightfall, and would have to return the

next day to collect their bounty. According to medieval lapidaries, peridot set in gold banished nightmares, while when strung on donkey's hair and worn as a bracelet on the left arm, it would drive away evil spirits.

Magic use

A fabulous stone for spells and rituals to reawaken your true purpose, bring you clarity or help you manifest your dreams. In grids, peridot boosts any form of manifestation, and when placed in the home, it strengthens your resolve and encourages vitality and quick thinking. In divination, a positive placement indicates that it's time to study your true mission in life, and that you will be rewarded. In a blockage position, it shows that you may be trying too hard to control your life, thus creating tension and negative influence.

Libra

Qualities: generous, entertaining, fair, compassionate, forgiving, loving, indecisive

Blue sapphire

Keywords

Integrity, fidelity, harmony, wisdom, empowerment, good fortune.

Healing use

Aids the thyroid and nervous system, and helps with blood disorders.

Chakras

Throat and brow.

Mystery and myth

A variety of corundum (ruby is red corundum), the blue sapphire has long been one of the most desirable gemstones in the world. It was worn by ancient pharaohs as protection against all evil and to attract the beneficial power of the gods. In medieval times, the stone was valued by sorcerers for its ability to bestow the wearer with prophetic power, and for its efficacy as an antidote against poison. A thirteenth-century Scandinavian ring set with a sapphire is inscribed with the words, 'I am sapphire, I conquer poison'. When worn or carried, it was believed to open locked doors, both literally and metaphysically. According to various versions of the *Alexander Romance*, based on a third-century Greek quasi-historical manuscript about the life of Alexander the Great, while on his travels, Alexander saw palaces built with sapphire walls and climbed two thousand sapphire steps to reach the summit of Sri Pada (a mountain sacred to Buddha) in Sri Lanka. According to the mystic Hildegard of Bingen, if you licked a sapphire frequently, you would become shrewd and wise.

Magic use

Rough-cut blue sapphire is much more affordable than a cut gemstone, but take care to buy it from a genuine supplier. Use it in magic spells and rituals to empower you with integrity and to attract good fortune. Placed in the home, it will enhance fidelity, acceptance and understanding between you and your family. As an oracle stone, sapphire indicates success in any venture, or shows that new light will be shone on a confused situation. In a difficult divination placement, the stone asks you to stop always saying yes and to learn how to say no.

Scorpio

Qualities: determination, integrity, shrewdness, charisma, self-containment, passion

Obsidian

Keywords

Empowering, transformative, release from fear, deep truth, protection against negativity.

Healing use

Helps with arthritic joints and aids the digestive system.

Chakras

Root and sacral.

Mystery and myth

Note that there are various forms of obsidian, ranging from intense black to gold. Some forms have a silver-grey iridescent sheen; then there's the reddish-brown mahogany obsidian and the snowflake variety with white inclusions. Black obsidian was renowned as a scrying crystal in Mesoamerican traditions and in medieval Europe. The best-known scrying mirror was owned by Dr John Dee, a sixteenth-century magus and adviser to Queen Elizabeth I, who used his mirror to communicate with angels. The Aztecs carved images of their great sky god, Tezcatlipoca, from black obsidian, and also used the highly polished stone for weaponry and as mirrors for shamanic or prophetic rituals.

Magic use

Obsidian is a powerful protective stone when used in grids and spells. It can also be used to boost other crystals' powers, and as a standalone meditational or ritual stone when placed at the core of a grid. It can be used on its own with relevant herbs or symbols to promote protection against all psychic or electromagnetic negativity. In divination, a positive placement indicates a time of transformation and change; in a blockage position, it shows you that it's time to let go of old patterns of behaviour.

Sagittarius

Qualities: adventurous, enthusiastic, spontaneous, optimistic, open-minded, impulsive

Turquoise

KEYWORDS
Good fortune, ambition, protection, safe travel, wisdom, self-assurance.

HEALING USE
Aids the immune system, vitalises the metabolism, and helps with respiratory disorders.

CHAKRAS
Throat and heart.

MYSTERY AND MYTH
Ancient Persian warriors hung turquoise amulets on their horse's bridles to protect against evil. It was believed that if the horse fell, both rider and mount would be miraculously unharmed. The Native American peoples, particularly in the south-west, regarded the stone as sacred to the Great Spirit, a mysterious creator god. Placed in burial chambers to protect the soul, it was an essential magic talisman for shamanic work and protection against harm. The Apache peoples prized turquoise as a sacred thunder stone. Legend has it that if a hunter stood

at the end of a rainbow after a thunderstorm, they would find a piece of turquoise in the earth directly beneath them (if they looked carefully enough), which would give them the power of perfect aim while hunting.

Magic use

Turquoise is a good luck stone, bringing success, creativity, truth and wisdom to the wearer. When used in spells or rituals related to your financial well-being or career, it promotes ambition and positive results. When used as a talisman or worn as an amulet, it protects travellers and helps with all forms of negotiation. When in a positive placement in a divination reading, turquoise indicates success is in sight. In a blockage position, it suggests that before making a decision, it's best to listen to the advice of trustworthy friends.

Capricorn

Qualities: responsible, committed, ambitious, organised, loyal, prosperous

Ruby

Keywords

Wealth, power, abundance, protection, security, invincibility.

Healing use

Aids circulation, stimulates the metabolism and promotes sexual vitality.

Chakra

Base.

Mystery and myth

One of the four most precious stones in the world – the others being diamond, emerald and sapphire – the ruby was sometimes confused with garnet and spinel (other varieties of red stone), until, in 1800, it was discovered to be a red variety of corundum (all other corundums are now known as sapphires in their different colourings). Historically, the ruby has been highly desired by kings and queens, thanks to the belief that it would bestow great wealth upon the wearer or owner. Highly valued as a precious and sacred gem by the Hindus, the ruby was believed to have four distinct classes or castes. The possession of the most precious ruby, *padmaraga*, meaning 'red as the lotus', would protect the owner from all misfortune. Medieval lapidaries also tell of the stone's powers to protect from enemies and witchcraft, and even its ability to guard fruit trees and vines against storms.

Magic use

Rough rubies are a little more expensive than many other stones, but are readily available. When worn as a talisman or charm, rubies can promote a sense of self-empowerment and invincibility, protecting you from all kinds of outer stress and inner demons. The belief that an inextinguishable flame burns in the centre of a ruby can be used symbolically in spells to bring to life creative ideas, promote professional success, and restore ardour between lovers. In divination, a well-placed ruby denotes abundance to come or inner richness, while in a blockage position, it suggests that you may be too power-hungry or over-zealous to achieve a goal.

Aquarius

Qualities: open-minded, visionary, free-spirited, humanitarian, changeable, quirky

Amber

KEYWORDS
Protection, detox, absorbs negativity, good luck, release from fear.

HEALING USE
Reduces pain and inflammation; relieves emotional stress.

CHAKRAS
Solar plexus and sacral.

MYSTERY AND MYTH
Formed from fossilised pine resin over millions of years, I have associated this unusual 'stone' with Aquarius

because it is not formed in the same way as the other stones in this book. Aquarius is a sign of non-conformity, rebellion, difference, so the stone's origins speak to this. As the pine resin dripped down the tree trunk, it might have enveloped insects, bits of other plants, hairs and so on, trapping them in its viscous liquid. When the trees fell due to geological stresses, they were carried down to the sea where they may have lain for thousands of years before the amber was found. So, like Aquarius, amber is unique – and, like Aquarius, its magic draws you out of yourself, releases you from inhibitions and fears. It challenges traditional assumptions of what a 'stone' is, and brings you luck.

Magic use

This is one of the best protective stones to simultaneously draw out negativity from mind, body, spirit and soul – but make sure it's 'real' amber. It should warm up when placed in the palm of your hand. Wear as jewellery to free you from negative thoughts and overthinking; place in the home to help detox the space and remove geopathic stress. In divination, amber in a positive placement indicates you can now manifest a dream; in a blockage position, it shows that you need to free yourself from emotional baggage before you can move on.

Pisces

Qualities: imaginative, intuitive, generous, understanding, creative, elusive, psychic

Amethyst

KEYWORDS
Calming, boosts the spirit, amplifies positive vibes, connection.

HEALING USE
Used for detoxification, and aids the nervous system and immune system. Has a calming effect.

CHAKRAS
Crown and third eye.

MYSTERY AND MYTH
Apart from the ancient belief that it could cure drunkenness and excessive lust, amethyst has been used throughout history as a stone to protect against evil, negativity and danger, and to improve the mind. In the sixteenth century, French poet Remy Belleau authored a work titled 'L'Amethyste, ou les Amours de Bacchus et d'Amethyst', detailing the story of Bacchus, the Greek god of wine and pleasure, and a mortal named Amethyst. After being spurned by a nymph, a furious Bacchus vowed to condemn the next person he met to the gruesome fate of being

devoured by tigers. The unlucky maiden Amethyst was on her way to worship at Diana's temple when she happened upon Bacchus. As the tigers sprang, Amethyst called on Diana for mercy and was immediately transformed into a pure white stone and saved. Realising the cruelty of his terrible curse, Bacchus poured some of his wine over the white stone as a libation to pacify his guilt, and the stone was turned to the violet hue it is known for today. In the days of courtly love, it was believed that if a knight spoke the name of the lady he desired directly to an amethyst, she would fall in love with him.

Magic use

Amethyst is a superb stone to use for spells where you want to boost your creative or imaginative powers. Use during the dark of the new moon to put an end to all past hurts and fears. It is a powerful stone in rituals for letting go and relinquishing or curing addictive habits. In a positive position in divination, it signifies a time for re-evaluation, creative endeavour and connecting to your deepest desires. In a blockage position, it suggests that your imagination is working overtime and you need to be more logical.

A ritual to prepare planet and zodiac crystals

This simple ritual will prepare you to connect to the planetary and zodiac energies associated with each planet so that you can befriend and make use of them more easily.

You will need:

the five element stones (pages 51–58)
the three power stones (pages 58–59)
the planet or zodiac crystal(s) you have selected

1. Make a grid from the five element stones. Place the Spirit stone in the centre, with the four elements surrounding it in a circle: Water to the north, Fire to the south, Air to the east and Earth to the west.
2. Use the three power stones to mark out a large triangle around the circle. The focus stone should be at the highest point, the guide stone to the lower left, and the protection stone to the right.
3. Take your planetary crystal(s) and place in the palm of your hand, holding your hand above the central Spirit stone. (If you can't fit them all in your hand at the same time, do several at a time.)
4. Repeat the following (for each crystal if you hold them separately):

'This Spirit strong connects to you
My crystal friend(s) of planets new
To guide, protect, or be my eyes
Now with my stones I will be wise.'

5. Your planet and zodiac crystals have now been charged with your personal energy and are ready to work with you for beneficial results, whether in divination, spell work or healing and protection.

Choosing crystals by colour

If you haven't been able to collect all the stones mentioned above, don't worry. Here are some examples of stones that can be used as alternatives:

Blue stones

For spiritual healing, peace and self-understanding:

- Blue lace agate – clarity
- Lapis lazuli – wisdom/truth
- Aquamarine – intuition
- Topaz – self-realisation

Red and orange stones

For power, getting things done, action and courage:

- Ruby – passion, conviction
- Red jasper – results, success, taking action
- Goldstone – wealth, charisma
- Sunstone – inspiration, achievement, consolidation

Purple stones

For imagination, mystery and psychic power:

- Sugilite – inner connection, spiritual revelation
- Purple sapphire – awareness, awakening
- Charoite – transformation, universal love
- Purple fluorite – mysteries revealed, psychic ability

Pink stones

For harmony, true love, self-worth and acceptance:

- Rose quartz – romance, new love, peace
- Rhodochrosite – self-acceptance, togetherness, loyalty
- Pink tourmaline – harmony, self-worth, giving, receiving
- Pink amethyst – truth, romantic intention, reconciliation

Yellow stones

For clarity, intention, focus, joy and brightness:

- Citrine – prosperity, mindfulness, optimism
- Yellow sapphire – opportunity, reward, inner wealth
- Yellow fluorite – quick thinking, beneficial ideas
- Orange calcite – intellectual power

Green stones

For manifestation, progress, ambition and material success:

- Jade – financial success, luck, decision-making
- Green tourmaline – financial results, focus, reward
- Malachite – material abundance, security, progress
- Serpentine – prosperous power, leadership, goal-setting

Black and brown stones

For stability, empowerment and resilience:

- Mahogany obsidian – self-confidence, material gain
- Jet – protection, balance, certainty
- Onyx – Strength, potency, self-control
- Black tourmaline – grounding, protection, safe action

White, clear and opaline stones

For insight, illumination, self-awareness and wisdom:

- Clear quartz – amplification of desires, revelation of truth
- White topaz – truth, clarity, peace of mind
- White agate – level-headedness, resolve, logical reflection

- White labradorite – flexibility, confidence, good luck

Part three will show you how to put all of this knowledge into practice. The spells, charms and rituals in this section will enable you to connect to the magic of crystals, and allow you to manifest you goals, wishes and desires.

PART THREE

Magic Spells, Rituals, Charms and Practices

Now that you have gathered a collection of personal crystals that are precious to you, you can start to make some magic in your life. Making things happen requires intention, belief and action, followed by manifestation. So before you set off casting spells, you need to ground yourself, promote belief in your ingredients and your power, and know what it is you are seeking. What are your goals? What are your motives for casting a spell? Most of all, remember that when you cast a spell, you are doing so for the good of all: for the universe and everything in it, which, of course, includes you.

Grounding ritual

Crystals are born of the earth itself, and so this ritual will help you to connect to their natural source and ground you, enabling you to successfully work with their magic.

You will need:

a glass bowl filled with water
the five element crystals (clear quartz, malachite, opal, fire agate, kyanite)
a handful of fresh or dried lavender
a white candle

1. This ritual is best performed in an outside space so that you can align more directly to the energies of the earth beneath, around and above you. Place the bowl of water on the ground, then gently place each of the crystals in the bowl.
2. As you do so, say:

   'With crystals five I find my ground,
   With Fire and Earth, I'm glory bound,
   With Water, Air, I'm here to be,
   While Spirit guides the best of me.'

3. Sprinkle the lavender into the bowl, then hold the candle up to the sky (you don't have to light it, as it is the symbolic act that matters). As you do so, say:

   'I am now grounded and charged with
   practised power
   Connected to Mother Nature, I work her
   crystal tower.'

4. Leave the crystals and bowl overnight. In the morning, rinse your crystals in spring water and return them to your chosen place. You are now grounded and can be sure of working seriously with your desires and intentions – but first, you need to know what those are.

Intention Visualisation

This ritual ensures that you become aware of your true intentions and desires. It's all very well hoping that things will happen, but if you don't actually know what you want, then the universe won't be able to oblige either. This ritual will help you to focus on your goal with clarity and purpose.

You will need:

a piece of clear quartz

1. Find a quiet, relaxed place to perform this visualisation. Hold the crystal between both hands, so its energy flows through the circuit that is you. Concentrate on the crystal. If you like, you can repeat: *'I hold this crystal, it is my intention,'* until you are in a calm, still state.
2. Now turn your focus away from the crystal and towards your intention or goal. Make sure you are very clear what this intention is. You can write down a specific goal before you start the ritual, such as 'I want to change my lifestyle' or 'I want to travel'. Focus for a minute or so on your intention.
3. Visualise yourself in a certain landscape, or with certain types of people, doing things you like to do. Whatever your intention, make it vivid and real in your mind. Your imagination is the conduit to the deeper unconscious part of your mind that

is connected to the magic of the universe. If you believe and imagine this reality often enough, the intention will manifest.

4. You now need to seal your intention as a sign to the universe. Although the enchantment or spell will usually reinforce your intention by its very practice, you need to speak it from the heart and soul too. Simply take up your crystal again between both hands. Relax and close your eyes, then recite this affirmation:

'My intention is made clear and true to the universe, and its joy be shared with all.'

5. After you have performed this visualisation for the first time, turn your mind to ordinary things again, like doing the washing-up, to help bring you back to normality. When you have practised this a few times, you will be able to easily snap into 'intention mode' just before you begin any magic work.

Chapter 6

Crystal Rituals and Practices for Self-Empowerment

Self-empowerment isn't just about making yourself invincible, courageous or charismatic; it's also about harmonious living, accepting who you are, nurturing your mind, body and spirit, and caring about all aspects of yourself. To feel is to live, to breathe is to love, to express and receive is to be empowered. The rituals and charms in this chapter will promote not only a sense of purpose and determination, but also an enriched sense of being.

EMPOWERMENT LABYRINTH

The creation of an empowerment labyrinth is a pathway to accessing your deeper needs, helping you to better understand your intentions and desires.

In Greek mythology, the Cretan princess Ariadne gave the hero Theseus a ball of red thread so that, after destroying the dreaded Minotaur, he could find his way back out of the labyrinth. By taking this labyrinth journey, you'll be empowered – not as the hero Theseus, but as the rewarded Ariadne. Although Theseus would eventually betray her, Ariadne went on to become the wife of the god Dionysus, and her wedding crown was set in the heavens as the constellation Corona Borealis.

You can use as many stones and crystals as you like for your labyrinth: in fact, the more complex the labyrinth and the greater the variety of stones, the more effective and energising it will be. Make it visually striking: a bold, expressive design will help to symbolically activate the labyrinth and your connection to your inner self.

You will need:

a selection of stones and crystals: use as many wayside stones, pebbles or stones as you can find, and include a selection of palm stones, wands, tumbled stones, polished stones and planetary, zodiac or traditional crystals

1. To make your labyrinth, clear a large surface in

your garden or sanctuary where you can leave the labyrinth for as long as you require it. You can also leave it in a quiet spot in the countryside, if you are sure that no one else will find it and disturb it.

2. Start with one central stone, then gradually place others in two close parallel lines, spreading out and around, perhaps like a spiral, or resembling a square maze. Don't stop to think about this too much; just let it flow. Let the stones tell you where they want to be placed: if you are in tune with them, they will be in tune with you.
3. When you have created your labyrinth, sit beside it for a few minutes and say:

   'Labyrinth of stones set fast out here
   To bring me knowledge loud and clear
   Of who I am and where I've been
   This labyrinth path is now serene.'

4. Reflect on how you started at its centre. Have you forgotten who you were then, just a few minutes or so ago? Or can you clearly recall the moment you placed your first stone? How did it feel? Who were you then? How did it feel when you placed your last stone? Who are you now?
5. With your finger, begin to find your way back into the labyrinth, touching as many stones as you can on your journey. Once you've found the centre again, work your way back out. Now that you have symbolically walked the labyrinth, you will

be aware that there is a way into the deep darkness inside yourself, and that you can always return from it to the light of day.

6. Leave the labyrinth in place for at least one lunar cycle, and you will be empowered and revitalised.

Bloodstone Good Fortune Enchantment

We all want some good fortune in our lives. This simple charm will enhance all favourable encounters, banish deceptive influences and put your life back on track with passion or purpose.

You will need:

a bowl of water
3 x 15cm (6in) pieces of string, twine or thread, each with 3 knots tied along its length
3 bloodstones

1. On the night of a new crescent moon, place the bowl of water on your sacred altar, then lay the three knotted strings around it to form a triangle facing north.
2. One at a time, drop the bloodstones gently into the bowl of water. Listen to the sound each makes as it plops through the water. In Celtic folklore, bloodstone was thought to speak and reveal your luck when submerged in water!
3. Once the three bloodstones are in the water, say:

'I stand my ground with bloodstones found
And from this day I will be heard
For fortune's sake or deeds be done
To bring me all that I deserve.'

4. Leave in place until the full moon, and you will soon be blessed with good luck.

Enhanced effects

To enhance this spell for specific desires, use the bloodstone's traditional magical influence on the weather. For example, perform this spell outside on a windy day to invoke surprise and change, on a rainy day to wash away sadness, on a sunny day to promote passion in your life, or on a still, windless day to finalise a deal.

TURQUOISE AND AMBER SELF-ACCEPTANCE RITUAL

Turquoise is a stone of vitality, while amber is one of revival and willingness. To aid us in our quest for self-empowerment, we need to learn to humbly accept who we are and the fact that we are only human. Once we stop judging ourselves and see our own unique character with all its qualities, both good and not so good, we can begin to feel truly empowered. This simple ritual will reinforce that sense of self-awareness whenever you need a boost.

You will need:

3 basil leaves
a lidded jar
3 pieces of turquoise
3 pieces of amber

1. This is best performed on a night between the new crescent moon and the full moon. Place the basil leaves in the jar (to protect and nurture your spirit), then close the lid and surround the jar with the six crystals in an alternating pattern.
2. Now take up each stone in your hand, one at a time, as you say:

   'This stone will bring me acceptance of self,
   This stone will bring me a sense of wealth,
   To know myself best is to love and to care
   For all of the universe blessed right from here.'

3. Once you have repeated this six times, place the crystals in the jar, then close the lid and leave them in place overnight to energise your ritual for self-acceptance.
4. The next morning, take one of the crystals and carry it with you all day. You will immediately feel or sense a difference about yourself. Note how you are less judgemental, more able to accept yourself and others too.
5. You can leave this as a grid in your home. When

the basil wilts, throw the leaves away. The stones will be energised for one lunar cycle, so during this time you can still pick one crystal and carry it with you whenever you need a self-esteem boost. Repeat the spell at the next new crescent moon to re-energise the stones' special powers.

Aventurine Inspirational Progress Spell

When we feel glad to be alive, excited, inspired and goal-oriented, we are at last making progress towards achieving or fulfilling a desire. But to kick-start that sense of progress, we may also need a little help from the universe. This spell will invoke motivation and sparkle into your life.

You will need:

a handful of fresh or dried rosemary sprigs
a handful of fresh or dried sage leaves
2 pieces of green aventurine
a container

1. Place the rosemary, sage and green aventurine in your container and go outside.
2. Seek out a plant that you feel a connection with and sit beside it. Now carefully take out the two stones without spilling your herbs. Place the stones either side of your chosen plant and chant these words:

'By green of life and green of stone
I make my way this path be known,
And all that will be sent to me
A road to progress, let it be.'

3. You can now turn your container upside down and let the herbs fall freely on the ground before you. This is a dedication to the uplifting energy of nature and will inspirit you with motivation and enthusiasm for all future ventures.
4. Remove your stones and thank nature for its energy and kindness.

Obsidian restorative ritual

As a child, it's likely that you played the game Rock, Paper, Scissors – here is a new take on it. This ritual will bless you with the restorative power of obsidian, to cut through all negativity and to lighten your spirit.

You will need:

a piece of obsidian
a piece of paper
scissors

1. Preferably on the night of the full moon, take the obsidian and wrap it in the paper. Hold the tiny

package in your hands for a few minutes while you recite this incantation:

'Here lies a stone now wrapped in shade
To heal my spirit, blaze my name,
With one cut here, I'll free my soul,
Then take this crystal for my cure,
Restored and blessed, I'll love the stone
And place it by my bed at home.'

2. Now take your scissors and cut through the paper – avoiding your crystal, of course. This will allow you to win obsidian's protective, cutting, no-nonsense influence. Remove the crystal and place it beneath your pillow or beside your bed. By the morning, all negative thoughts or feelings will melt away and you will feel restored and cared for.

Abundance and Achievement Spell

Abundance isn't just about how much money or how many possessions you have. It's also about how you feel inside. If you feel dissatisfied with life or live with a sense of emptiness, you may lack a connection to the abundant energies of the universe. This ritual will put you back in touch. If you are already motivated to achieve more in your life, this spell will work well for you, too.

You will need:

a piece of clear quartz
3 red stones
3 blue stones
3 yellow or orange stones
3 green stones
cedarwood essential oil

1. On a new crescent moon night, place the crystals on your sacred space or altar and sit quietly for a few moments while you reflect on what kind of abundance or achievement you're seeking. Remember, don't just think 'to get more money' or 'to get noticed' or 'to achieve more' – be explicit and clear. Say how much money (within reason), or who you want to be noticed by, or what sort of achievement you are seeking exactly.
2. Now take the quartz crystal and place it to mark a central point. Make a circle of blue stones around it, followed by a circle of red, then yellow, then green. Focus on the magic circles of stones as you say:

   'These blue stones bring me deep desires,
   While red the cause to fan my fires,
   Then yellow, green to ground my deeds,
   Abundant quartz achieves my needs.'

3. Consecrate each stone with a tiny drop of

cedarwood essential oil to seal your intention to the universe, then leave overnight. Remove your stones in the morning and keep them in a safe place for one lunar cycle to activate the abundance you are seeking.

RITUAL TO PROTECT YOU FROM ENVY OR NEGATIVE PEOPLE

The ancient Greeks believed opals and clear quartz crystals bestowed the wearer with the gift of invisibility. Although we don't necessarily want to disappear into thin air, there are times we need to feel invisible and protected from people who might project their negative thoughts or feelings on to us. This ritual will cloak you in invisibility when you need it.

You will need:

a piece of clear quartz or opal
a piece of red carnelian
a piece of blue lace agate
a piece of citrine
a piece of malachite
your focus stone (see page 59)

1. With your focus stone on the table in front of you, take up the red carnelian (which represents the element Fire) and say:

'From Fire to Fire, this stone is set
To burn away those who negate.'

2. Repeat this five times, then place the stone to the left of the focus stone and say:

   'With this stone, I am unconquerable.'

3. Pick up the blue lace agate (for Water) and say:

   'From Water to Water, this stone is mine
   To keep me from harm of any kind.'

4. Repeat five times, then place to the right of the focus stone. Say:

   'With this stone, I am cloaked in dark and light.'

5. Pick up the citrine (for Air) and say:

   'From Air to Air, my spirit's safe
   And none can hurt nor break my faith.'

6. Place it above the focus stone, and repeat five times:

   'With this stone, I am hidden'.

7. Take up the malachite (for Earth), and say:

'From Earth to Earth, my will be done
And hold my strength that All is One.'

8. Place to the south of the focus stone and repeat five times:

   'With this stone, I am resilient.'

9. Finally, place the clear quartz next to the focus stone, and repeat five times:

   'I am as clear as this crystal, and invisible to all
   who would project their negativity on to me.'

10. Leave overnight to inspirit your intention with lunar and solar power. Now you can go out into the world and sense an invisible light of pure crystal energy surrounding you, protecting you from negative people.

RED CARNELIAN TALISMAN FOR FUN AND PASSION IN YOUR LIFE

Sometimes, we don't want to achieve, work, plan ahead, economise or even make an effort. We just want to have fun, enjoy, play, flirt, smile and take life less seriously. Here's a lovely way to rediscover the carefree spirit in you or attract some 'spice' into your world.

You will need:

a red candle
5 red carnelians (or rough rubies)
5 large red rose petals
ylang ylang essential oil

1. On a waxing moon night, light the candle and place your ingredients in front of it. Line up the five stones from left to right and intersperse them with the five rose petals. Drip one drop of the essential oil on to each petal.
2. Now place each stone in the middle of a petal and, as you do so, say:

   'Take five red stones to stir my passion,
   Take five red flowers for satisfaction,
   Take oils of love and flames so bright,
   Enhance all joys with burning light.'

3. Focus on the crystals for a few moments and find stillness and calm. When you are ready to leave, blow out the candle and leave the crystals and flowers in place. The next day, take one red stone and carry it with you as a talisman to attract fun, lighten your spirit, and bring happiness.

   Swap your stone at the end of the day for another of the five and continue to do this for five days until each crystal has been used as a talisman. Respectfully bury or throw away the rose petals.

Continue to use the crystals as your talismans of passion whenever you need a boost of *joie de vivre.*

Tiger's eye and pomegranate seed shot of courage ritual

When you need a shot of courage, do you reach for the gin bottle, practise deep breathing or flip into warrior mode? Or do you find yourself holding your head in your hands and weeping? This little ritual will boost your innate qualities of bravery, audacity, grit and mettle when most needed, and give you the determination, nerve and strength to get through a difficult encounter or event.

You will need:

spring water
a small lidded jar
a handful of pomegranate seeds
a piece of tiger's eye
a bowl

1. Pour the spring water into the jar, and pop in as many pomegranate seeds as you can. Close the lid, shake the jar a little, and leave overnight to infuse.
2. The next day, place your tiger's eye in the bowl and pour the pomegranate elixir over it. Leave it for an hour or so, then remove the crystal and allow it to dry in a warm room or a sunny spot.

3. The crystal is now programmed and ready to give you courage. All you need do is place it to your forehead and focus on what you need your shot of courage for, and the crystal will animate you with bravado. Do this whenever you are faced with a difficult situation or problem.

Carpe Diem, or Seize an Opportunity with Aventurine

When faced with an exciting opportunity, many of us hesitate, reflect, worry and then miss the chance to change something for the better. This ritual will make it clear whether you should take the chance or not.

You will need:

3 pieces of green aventurine
3 sage leaves

1. Cup the three pieces of aventurine between both hands and focus on the opportunity in question. Imagine how it might enhance your life: will it improve your status, your emotional state, your love life, your work ethic, your moral strength? What will it improve in your world?
2. Now imagine how the opportunity could negatively impact your life. Will it mean you lose a pal, freedom, self-belief, money? Once you have

considered how the opportunity will impact you, both positively and negatively, wrap each piece of aventurine in a sage leaf. Take each one in turn and hold it just below your navel (the centre of all energy flow, known as the *hara*) and say:

'To take this chance is my delight
To know it's worth my personal right
To take it now and seize the day
Or drop all thoughts and walk away.'

3. After you have repeated this three times, you will know the right thing to do, thanks to the power of each crystal connecting to your deeper self. Then it's your choice whether to seize the day or forget it. Throw away the sage leaves and keep these crystals separate from all the others, as they are now programmed for any further decisions you need to make.

Peridot determination ritual

This lovely soft green stone is perfect for focusing your mind and strengthening your will when combined with the powerful influence of the mighty oak tree. This ritual is best carried out on a windy day at the end of autumn or in early winter, when oak leaves have fallen to the ground and you can collect them. However, if you don't live in the right habitat for oak trees, or you need this boost of determination out of season, then you can either cut out photos of oak leaves from magazines or sketch some yourself in order to feel in touch with the tree's power.

You will need:

a handful of oak leaves
a small container
2 pieces of peridot

1. Place your oak leaves in the container and find an outdoor space. Once you are outside, stand facing into the wind and hold a crystal in each hand. Raise your arms to the sky and say:

   'With the power of oak and peridot, I am determined to make my way, and nothing will stop me from achieving my goals.'

2. Then place the crystals on the ground, open your container and shake the leaves into the wind so that they will be blown behind you. Wait for twenty seconds, or until you feel sure the leaves have settled on the ground. Then take up the two crystals again and, holding them close to your forehead, turn your back to the wind and say:

   'With my eye I see the way,
   With this wind my fears allayed,
   With this stone my hope is made,

With this stone I see a glade
Of scented woods where celandine
Grows low beneath sweet eglantine.
Take oak leaves thrown against the breeze
To cast my spell for power to seize.'

3. Pick up the oak leaf nearest to you and place it in the container, along with your crystals. (If you have used paper leaves, make sure to collect all of them before leaving.) Keep the container under your bed overnight and you will be blessed with the resoluteness and decisiveness of the mighty oak.

Double lunar ritual for self-belief

These two spells work best when performed during the same lunar cycle, as the full moon spell reinforces the power of the new crescent moon spell.

New moon spell

You will need:

2 selenite wands
2 pieces of red carnelian

1. During the evening of a new crescent moon, take the stones and settle into a comfortable, seated

position, outside or indoors. It doesn't matter if you can't see the moon: its influence is still there. Make your intention known to the universe by saying:

'Thank you, the moon this night, for blessing me with self-belief.'

2. With a selenite wand in each hand, raise your arms above your head in salutation of the new crescent moon. As you do so, say:

   'My purpose now is self-belief
   To know my truth and live it true
   These stones will bring me lunar light
   And cast my soul's esteem so bright.'

3. Place the wands on the ground, then pick up the two pieces of red carnelian. Hold them close to your sacral chakra for a moment and imagine the colour red permeating your whole body to give you the gift of confidence and purpose. Come out of your visualisation and leave all the crystals exposed to the evening sky (either outside or inside on a window ledge) for one night to be charged with lunar power.

Full moon spell

You will need:

the selenite wands and pieces of red carnelian
from the last ritual
a moonstone
a piece of clear quartz

1. On the evening of the full moon, take the selenite, carnelian, moonstone and quartz and stand outside where you can look up at the sky. Place all the stones on the ground, except the moonstone, which you should hold high above your head as you say:

   'Fulfil this deed for self-belief
   With stones as pure as golden leaf
   For now, my soul is filled with trust
   So, mind and spirit are stardust.
   Thank you, crystals and the moon, for energising
   my spirit and soul.'

2. Leave the crystals under the evening sky (or inside on a window ledge) overnight and you will wake up the next day with a real sense of purpose, self-belief and renewed confidence.

Talisman for Self-Love

This simple charm will always remind you to love yourself and not to give your love away too freely.

You will need:

a pink or red rose
rosewater or rose essential oil
a piece of ruby
a small pouch

1. Place the rose on a flat surface and sprinkle the rosewater or rose essential oil over the flower to consecrate it. Next, take the ruby and place it gently in the middle of the rose. Again, sprinkle either a little rosewater or a drop of rose essential oil on the crystal.
2. Now say:

'With rose and ruby, love be found
That love is mine and mine all round
To love my north, south, east and west
And give myself a world that's blessed.'

3. Put the ruby in the pouch and carry it with you all day to promote and enhance all aspects of self-love – which helps others love you, too.

Malachite ritual for setting personal boundaries

Apart from protecting ourselves from negativity and empowering ourselves with love and belief, we also need to learn to set boundaries. In other words, to not give others the chance to cross the line, manipulate us, or impose their beliefs or expectations on us. It's really about learning to say 'no', or even 'let me think about it', and then giving yourself the chance to make your own decision. Many of us tend to say 'yes' because we think it means we will be accepted or liked, but being a people-pleaser comes at a high price.

This ritual will help you set personal boundaries so that you can stop saying yes, and can instead have the freedom to make your own choice.

You will need:

a piece of rose quartz
3 pieces of malachite
3 acorns
20cm (8in) length of string, cord, ribbon or twine

1. This spell is best performed on the evening of a waning moon. First, take your rose quartz crystal and place it on a flat surface where it won't be disturbed. Then take your three pieces of malachite and place them in a triangular formation around the rose quartz. Finally, form a second, outer triangle with the acorns.

2. Now turn your attention to the string. Make three, equidistant knots along the string, reciting the following spell as you do so:

   'This knotted twine it seals my mind,
   The first to bind my word to thine,
   The second hold the answer back
   To know that 'no' can now be said,
   The third to know what's true to me,
   So bind this twine and let it be.'

3. Now lay the string around your acorns to form a complete circle. Leave this in place for one lunar cycle to seal your intention for others to respect your boundaries and to confirm your ability to say 'no'.

Wisdom and Illumination Bath or Shower Elixir

Relaxing in a bath can be a blissful way to find peace of mind, helping to restoring your spirit and perhaps even letting you experience moments of enlightenment. If you don't have a bath, a shower can have the same effect. This elixir will refresh and vitalise your mind, brighten your world and bestow you with a positive and savvy outlook.

You will need:

4 pieces of red carnelian

4 red tea-light candles
2 handfuls of fresh flower petals (any kind you like, but preferably scented)
lemon or other citrus essential oil
5 yellow or orange flowers
frankincense incense

1. Begin by placing a piece of red carnelian and a tea-light at each corner of your bath. Then run the bath and, once it's ready, light the candles. Scatter the fresh petals and the five flowers across the surface of the water. (If you're showering instead, place the candles and the pieces of red carnelian in a group near the shower, and scatter the flowers around them.)
2. Light the incense and enjoy the atmosphere of your ritual. Spend as long as you like in your bath or under the shower. You will begin to tune in to a new part of your mind: the part concerned with imagination and intuition. Visualise yourself in a field of flowers: here you are all-seeing and wise, and can observe life from a new perspective.
3. After your bathing ritual, you will feel revitalised and have greater insight into what you want from your life, empowering you with self-awareness and wisdom.

Chapter 7

Crystal Rituals and Practices for Serenity

What is serenity? Rooted in ancient Latin and Greek words meaning dry, clear, calm and tranquil, the word 'serene' was first associated with calm or unclouded weather in the sixteenth century CE.

Self-empowerment and serenity aren't mutually exclusive: in fact, they are interdependent on one another. Feeling empowered is also about how comfortable you feel, both with yourself and with the world at large. Are you 'unclouded' by judgements, demands and other people's needs? Are you able to let go of anger, deal with difficult feelings, and stay calm when all around you are losing the plot? These rituals will help you to find the peace of your inner self, connect to that place and feel serenely empowered.

Lapis Lazuli Truth Spell

Having a goal, ambition or mission in life is one thing, but is that goal really the truth of who you are? Is that intention generated by the 'unclouded' you? Are you deceiving yourself about your desires, or are others deceiving you? Are other people's expectations not in keeping with your own sense of who you are? This ritual will enable you to see beyond the veil or fog of any illusion or deception and 'know thyself'.

You will need:

a white candle
5 pieces of lapis lazuli
5 fresh or dried lavender sprigs
lavender essential oil

1. On the night of a full moon, light the candle and place the five pieces of lapis in a horizontal line before you. Place a sprig of lavender beside each stone and a drip a drop of oil on to each crystal to seal your intention to the universe.

2. Now say:

   'To see the truth and know the way,
   I'll cast this spell for just a day.
   By powers of lapis, one to five
   There will I know which are my lies;
   From five to one, I'll see what's true
   And know my quest with stones so blue.'

3. Pick up the last piece of lapis and place it to the left of the first piece. Repeat this action five times, until the stones are back in their original order. As you move each stone, repeat the above incantation.
4. Holding the first stone in your hand, close your eyes and imagine a cloudless sky. You will feel yourself connecting to the truth. Say:

   'The truth is mine; I will make destiny
   all my own.'

5. After you have performed this ritual, you will be able to clearly see whether any project, ambition or plan is about you and your individuality, or someone else's.

Patchouli and Amethyst Elixir for Peaceful Sleep

If you're hoping to have pleasant dreams and a lovely nurtured feeling when you wake up in the morning, then try this amethyst bathing ritual, which will promote a good night's sleep.

You will need:

patchouli essential oil or perfume
4 pieces of amethyst
a piece of rose quartz
a piece of purple fluorite
2 tea-light candles

1. Run a bath and place a piece of amethyst at each corner around the bathtub. The rose quartz should be positioned near your head and the fluorite by your feet. Place the two candles by your feet as well, then drop as much patchouli oil or perfume as you like into the water. Step into the bath, then lie back and relax.
2. Now put the amethyst crystals into the water, placing one on either side of you, the third between your feet and the last between your thighs, as close to your base chakra as possible. Soak up their calming, restful energy for at least ten minutes.
3. Once you have taken your bath, carefully dry the stones, and place them under your pillow or bed

to reinforce their restorative qualities throughout the night.

Citrine and Chamomile Tea Ceremony to Encourage Healthy Friendships

Our friends offer us their support, and in turn we give ours back. But when we are lacking in people that we can count on – this might be due to moving to a new city, entering a new phase of life, or changing outlooks – we have to reach out to make new pals. There is, of course, a risk involved: will they be loyal? Can we trust them? To ensure you meet people who will lift you up, perform this tea ceremony before any social encounters with new people.

You will need:

chamomile tea
a white candle
2 pieces of citrine

1. Prepare your tea and light your candle. Settle down and relax. When the tea is cool enough to drink, begin to sip it slowly.
2. Pause and take a piece of citrine in each hand. Close your eyes and imagine these are two new friends, sociable, charming, and trustworthy. Hold the stones for a few minutes, then place one on each side of the candle and continue drinking your tea.

3. When you have finished your cup, take up your two crystals again and recite the following verse to attract beneficial strangers into your life:

   'They say they came from golden hills
   Where all soft citrine filled their ears
   Who sang a song of joyful note
   And brought their souls to be so near.
   So take these crystals in my hands
   A tea of herbs to cross this land
   To breezes speak and chant my time
   Of words that formed an ancient rhyme
   And last the golden crystals true
   Will say, good friends will come to you.'

4. Take your two citrine crystals with you to any new social occasion to bestow their energy upon you and to help you attract the kind of positive attention that you truly deserve.

Rose quartz well-being ritual

We experience calm and serenity when we live in the moment, when things don't 'matter too much', and we are more laid-back, light-hearted and easy-going. To attract beneficial energy for all-round holistic health, perform this lunar ritual every new crescent moon to boost the well-being of your mind, body and spirit.

You will need:

3 basil leaves
a piece of green tourmaline
a large piece of rose quartz (the larger the better)

1. Take the basil leaves and green tourmaline and bury them beneath a tree or in a pot on your terrace. As you bury the tourmaline, say:

   'With rose and green I will be seen
   Complete and good right through,
   This basil sweet brings nature's treat
   To make my soul renewed.'

2. Finally, place the rose quartz beside the pot or lay it on the surface of the soil above the buried tourmaline to invoke well-being and balance your energy levels. Leave in place until the full moon, then remove both the crystals and dispose of the basil. You will now be blessed with a purified sense of being.

Aquamarine Calming Ritual

When you want to thoroughly relax and put your feet up, this simple ritual will invite peace and stillness. Aquamarine is known for its ability to reduce stress, ease the mind and promote spiritual connection.

You will need:

3 pieces of aquamarine

1. Try to find somewhere comfortable where you can lie flat on your back to conduct this spell. Once you're in position, place the stones on your forehead, with one above the left eye, one above the right and one above the bridge of your nose. Leave for three minutes, and as you do so, say:

   'With these stones of softest blue
   I'm rested, still and tranquil too.
   Let go of all that stirs the soul
   To find repose wherever I go.'

2. Keep the aquamarines with you to promote calm whenever you need it.

Clear Quartz 'Get What You Wish For' Spell

Wishful thinking is one thing; making wishes come true is another. If we truly believe a wish will be fulfilled, then it will, but only if we are realistic about what it is that we want. So be careful to ensure your motives and intentions are as clear and as unclouded as the quartz you are about to use. Ancient Celtic folklore recommended kissing a quartz crystal when you made a wish to ensure its successful outcome, so you are going to do the same.

You will need:

a large piece of clear quartz
sandalwood essential oil

1. Focus for a minute or so on your wish. Imagine it coming true, and think about the consequences of making that wish. When you are absolutely clear and sure you want to go ahead, take the quartz in one hand. Dab a little of the sandalwood oil on your finger and trace your name on the crystal. You can then write one word that sums up your wish.
2. Now face west, and say:

   'What I wish for will be set in this stone.'

3. Turn east and repeat the incantation, then turn south, then north, repeating it each time.
4. You may now kiss the crystal three times to seal your wish to the universe and the stone. Put the crystal in a safe place until your wish has come true.

Magic circle for banishing stress

To live a tranquil life, we want to eliminate daily stressors such as confrontation, endless demands or social expectations that we can't live up to. Then, of course, there's also our inner anger, regrets, feelings of guilt, and all those 'if onlys' and 'what ifs'. This ritual can be performed just before you go out for the day to keep you calm and unruffled when faced with unprecedented circumstances or challenging experiences.

You will need:

5 pieces of amethyst
5 pieces of hematite
5 pieces of selenite
a pouch
a clear quartz wand or double-terminated crystal

1. Before you start your magic work, make sure you're in a space where you can surround yourself with the de-stressing stones on the floor. Start to lay the stones in an anti-clockwise direction, alternating amethyst, hematite, selenite and so on, until you have placed all the stones and made a complete circle around you. Hold your quartz wand and point it at each stone in turn, moving in a clockwise direction, and say to each stone:

'This magic takes all stress from me
I'm energised by stones that see.'

2. When you've connected to all fifteen stones, gather them into the pouch and you will quickly feel at ease with yourself and the world.
3. Repeat the above spell whenever you are in need of a de-stress session.

Tiger's Eye and Jade Positive-Thinking Spell

Being serene is also about the way we look at life. If we view a glass as half empty, we are thought to be pessimists; if we see a glass as half full, we are optimists. Some people believe that optimists will inevitably be let down, and so it's safer to be a pessimist. However, if we are steadfast in our belief that if we put out goodness, we will get some back, then the universe usually obliges. As the old saying goes, 'What goes around, comes around.'

This practice will enable you to restore positive thinking and shrug off any negative thoughts that come into your head. The more you practise this ritual, the easier it will become to adopt a positive mindset.

You will need:

a small empty glass

a handful of small tumbled, polished or rough pieces of green jade
3 pieces of tiger's eye

1. Place the glass on a surface, and position the three pieces of tiger's eye equidistantly around the glass.
2. Now pile the pieces of jade into the glass until it is half full. Gaze into the glass and say three times:

   'This glass is both half empty of jade and half full of jade, therefore it is a glass full of both.'

3. Now fill up the glass with the rest of the jade and say:

   'The glass is full of jade; it is always positive and brimming over with goodness.'

4. Place the tiger's eye crystals on top of the jade and leave it overnight.
5. Take at least one of the tiger's eye crystals with you wherever you go to remind you of the bountiful energy of the glass full of jade, and to promote optimism and positive thinking.

A RITUAL FOR DECISION-MAKING

This slightly longer ritual and the accompanying verse is for when you need to make an important decision about your future. It will help you truly believe in the universe and ensure that you make the right decision based on your circumstances. It will also promote peace of mind and give you a serene outlook on life.

You will need:

a piece of paper
4 birch leaves, or an image of a birch tree
4 pieces of green aventurine
4 pieces of black tourmaline

1. Outline the decision that you must make on a piece of paper, then place your birch leaves (or image of a birch tree) on top of the paper. Now arrange the aventurine in a horizontal line above the paper, and the black tourmaline in a line below it.
2. Pick up a piece of aventurine and say the first line of the verse below as you hold the stone. Return it to its place, then pick up a piece of black tourmaline and say the second line of the verse, and so on. When you get to the last four lines, pick up one birch leaf per line (or hold the image of the birch tree for all last four lines).

'In silken shoes and velvet beds
We find all life is made with threads.
Of golden sounds like honeyed dawn
When eyes of owls do cross the born.
If when you take both birch and stone
Then that's a song that's writ alone.

Then three of one and four of two
All twelve restore your mind to you.
From wilder places that we know
Of aged woods and darker groves
But finding truth among these ways
Now mark the path's decisive days.'

3. Once you have finished this ritual, leave the paper, leaves and crystals in place for a day and a night. At the end of the twenty-four hours, you will know exactly what your decision will be, and you'll have the motivation to put it into action.

Charisma talisman

Whether you're hoping to make new contacts, find romance or simply impress the world with your dazzling charisma, this talisman will bring out your flamboyant, hypnotic allure and make sure you attract the right kind of attention when you need it.

You will need:

a piece of rose quartz or rhodochrosite
a garnet
a piece of smoky quartz
lemon balm essential oil

1. On the evening of a new crescent moon, hold the rose quartz in one hand and the garnet in the other and say:

    'With these stones, charisma is mine,
    With oil of balm, I'll cross the line,
    With smoky quartz, my work be done,
    Then come enchanted with my sun.'

2. Place the rose quartz and garnet in front of you, and position the smoky quartz crystal between them so it can absorb the loving, harmonious energy of the pink crystals. Drizzle some of the lemon balm essential oil on the smoky quartz to seal your intention as you repeat the incantation above once more.
3. Take the smoky quartz with you wherever you go to charm and enchant others and ensure you always exude charisma. Recharge the stone by performing the same spell at each new crescent moon.

Witch Hazel and Moonstone Ritual to Ease the Pain of a Broken Heart

To help ease the pain of heartbreak, this ritual will give you the confidence and self-esteem you need to move forwards on a new journey and free yourself from the past.

You will need:

a white candle
a piece of moonstone
a piece of green tourmaline
a small glass bowl half-filled with witch-hazel water
jasmine essential oil
2m (6½ft) length of twine, string or ribbon

1. On the evening of a waning moon, light the candle and place the stones in the bowl of witch-hazel water. Add two drops of jasmine oil to the water to consecrate it and take up your length of twine. Tie twelve knots along the length of the twine, spacing them an even distance apart. Any old knots will do: it's the act of knotting that's important. When you have made twelve knots, hold each one in turn and repeat this incantation:

   'In moonlit caves she sat and waited
   For all that's wrong to be abated
   So fiercely gave her love to one
   Who shone the light from darker suns?
   Her moonstone heart so filled with laughter
   Her long-lost joy so filled with fear
   Lest all who touch its power are cast
   In glows of hazel's lightning fast.
   So take the stone and hold it close
   Wrap twine around to make it safe

Take tourmaline and jasmine binds
When candles lit will show the fires.
With stones now set in future's change
You'll braid the knots and free your chains.'

2. Remove the two stones from the water, place them on the table and encircle the crystals with the knotted twine.
3. On the evening of the new crescent moon, unwind your charm, and you will be free from your broken heart.

A SUNSTONE SALUTATION FOR A JOYFUL DAY

There are many traditional ways to give thanks to the power of our main life-giving force, the sun. This simple ritual will attract solar energy to boost your day and make it a happy one.

You will need:

a piece of sunstone

1. This spell is best conducted at sunrise, but if that's not possible, any time before noon will work. Sit crossed-legged or in a comfortable position facing the sun. Even if you can't see it, you can always work out where it is, because you know it rises to the east.

2. Place the sunstone before you and begin your practice. Raise your arms high above your head, palms touching in prayer, and hold this position for a few seconds before sweeping your arms down and round to form a prayer pose at your chest. After holding this position for a few seconds, raise your arms up again. Repeat this salutation ten times, all the while remembering to breathe rhythmically as you would in a yoga practice.
3. Place your hands on your knees to finish, then take up the sunstone and say:

'With this crystal charged, I embrace the sun's light to bring me a beautiful day.'

4. Take the sunstone with you for a beautiful day ahead.

AMETHYST CHARM TO AWAKEN YOUR SPIRITUAL SELF

Being serene in a spiritual sense isn't just about meditating; it's also about feeling that, deep within, you are in touch with your most secret self. Use this charm to awaken you to the soul of yourself, and make it a place of comfort, peace and harmony.

You will need:

2 white candles

a piece of amethyst
rose essential oil

1. On the night of a full moon, place the two candles 20cm (8in) apart and light them. Then take your amethyst and anoint it with a few drops of the rose oil before placing the stone between the two lit candles. Gaze into the flame of each candle for a minute or so, and then focus on the amethyst. As you do so, say:

   'This purple stone, it lights my way
   With rose to bring a moonlit day
   To show my self, to touch my soul
   Where peace is found and stillness gold.'

2. Blow out the candles and place the amethyst beside or under your bed to revive, restore and nourish your spirit and soul while you sleep.

Reconciliation Ritual with Rubies, Amber and Herbs

Whether you are hoping to get back with an ex or looking to mend a rift between you and a close friend or loved one, reconciliation is about mutual forgiveness and acceptance. This ritual will enhance all feelings of goodness between you. It may take one lunar cycle to work, but it will be worth the wait.

You will need:

a pile of tumbled, rough or wild stones
a handful of a mix of parsley, sage, thyme
and rosemary
4 pieces of ruby
4 pieces of amber
a piece of paper and a pen

1. This ritual is best performed on the evening of a new crescent moon. Take your wild stones and carefully pile them up to form a rough pyramid, with one stone resting on the top of the pile. If the stones topple, start again – this ritual is all about building and reshaping a relationship, after all.
2. Scatter the herbs around your pyramid to form a magic circle.
3. Place one ruby to the north of the pyramid, one to the south, one to the east and one to the west, then position your four pieces of amber between them so that the crystals form an alternating pattern.
4. Focus on your stone shrine. Think about the person you want to be reconciled with and why.
5. Now take the piece of paper and tear it in half. On the first half, write down the name of the person you have in mind. Fold the paper and place it under the ruby nearest to you. Write your own name on the other half of the paper, then fold it and place it under the ruby furthest from you.

6. Now repeat the following incantation:

   'Burning rubies in my soul
   Take me to some blackest hole
   Where stars shine bright beyond the clouds
   And crystals make us lost or found.
   Herb rosemary brings us memories
   While sage it unveils fantasies,
   Where parsley's sent to make us work
   And thyme's the twig to lessen hurt.
   Then amber gold you mix within
   To make a cure for all who spin,
   At last you take the red of love
   That's given in a velvet glove
   Then all the flames of love's desires
   Are written in your newfound fires.'

7. After one lunar cycle, at the next new crescent moon, remove the scraps of paper with the names and throw them away; disassemble the pile of stones and put them wherever you like. Keep the rubies and amber separately in a special place, and you will soon be reunited with your loved one.

Secret crystal pathway in nature ritual

If you have the inclination and a desire for a deeper connection to Earth magic and for being at one with nature, this ritual will not only fill you with a sense of being part of the universal adventure, but will also bring you the tranquillity that nature offers you. All you have to do is go out into the countryside to lay your trail.

The magic crystal trail is about connecting to the energies in nature, so with this in mind, you're going to engage with the five natural elements of Western magic that are found in nature that correspond to Fire, Earth, Air, Water and Spirit.

The Five Magical Elements

In the symbolic language of the magical elements, Fire corresponds to the landscape you see before you, whether it's the expanse of the horizon, a tangled patch of woodland, a vast forest, a lush valley, rolling hills or the vastness of the ocean. Fire is foresight, seeing, the journey ahead, so the landscape you see is the journey ahead of you.

Water is associated with the sacred spirituality of the planet and your connection to that sacredness. This includes both man-made spiritual sites, such as Stonehenge in the UK or the Nazca lines of Peru, as well as natural epicentres of sacred energy, such as Mount Fuji in Japan and Uluru in Australia. You may not have such a high-powered spiritual place close to home, but you will create one.

Earth corresponds to all that lives, including ourselves – but for the purposes of this ritual, it will point to flora and fauna: plants, trees, animals, insects, fish, coral and so on.

Air is associated with the sky, including the moon, the sun, the planets and constellations, as well as the weather.

The sky can send us storms, wind and rain; it can give us warm, pleasant days as well as cold, miserable ones, so the weather is an important aspect of Air.

Spirit is *you*. You are the quintessence, the pivotal force of the four other elements, and you will harness the magic of the other elements to create the nature trail and bring harmony for yourself and the planet.

You will need:

a rucksack or bag
a piece of paper and a pen
a piece of red carnelian (for Fire)*
a small spade
twine or string, cut into at least 5 x 20cm (8in) lengths
a selection of 10 tumbled, polished or natural crystals of your choice
a selection of 20 wild stones or pebbles
a piece of malachite (for Earth)*
a piece of citrine (for Air)*
a piece of amethyst (for Water)*
a piece of clear quartz (for Spirit)*

* Note: you will be burying these crystals, so don't choose ones that are too big or too precious.

The journey

Pack everything into your rucksack and bag and set off on a walk into nature. You might have already precisely planned your journey. You might already know how long it will take you; you may have plotted out the route on your GPS. However, on this walk (which I would personally take at a leisurely pace, aiming to walk for one to three hours), it may be that something catches your eye and you get led astray or wander off the route you have selected. You may find you are fascinated by something just over the hilltop that wasn't part of your original plan, or perhaps you will stop to observe an insect at work and find yourself caught in a downpour that means you have to take a more sheltered route. Whatever happens on your journey will reveal something about the journey itself and your personal quest to connect to nature. Make a note of these experiences, as you may find when you look back that these provide clues as to what your personal quest is really all about.

There are five rituals you need to perform that align to each of the elements. You can do the first four elements in any order, but you should always finish with the Spirit ritual so that your connection to the magic of nature will be assured.

The Fire ritual

1. While you're on your walk, look out for an area of natural beauty that is so breathtaking it makes you stop in your tracks. This might be a tranquil glade, a view of a mountain, or just a beach with crashing waves. I could go on, but it's up to you to make the ultimate choice. Remember that this is a place that will become very special to you. Whatever

inspires you, make a note of it on your piece of paper, remembering to write down exactly where you are (map coordinates, if you're savvy) so you can retrace your steps later.

2. When you have found your spot, take a moment to pause and catch your breath. Relax, sit down if you can, and focus on the Fire symbol before you. Hold the carnelian in your hands and then hold it above your crown chakra as you repeat the following:

   'With Fire I come with crystal fine
   To place in nature all that's mine
   I give this pledge of my esprit
   That from now on the Fire's in me.'

3. Dig a shallow, unobtrusive hole in the ground with your spade, and bury the crystal. If the earth is too hard for digging, you can hide the crystal under leaves, weeds, or stones. Encircle the burial place with a length of twine. Leave one of your ordinary stones or pebbles on the surface above as a marker too.
4. Bow to your Fire symbol and thank it for enabling you to connect to the magic in nature.

The Earth ritual

1. An Earth ritual can be performed at any moment you experience joy at meeting a creature great or small on your journey. It could be a butterfly,

a worm, a cow or a duck – or even a beautiful flower, a weed or the grass you walk across. Again, it is for you to decide. Whatever inspires your Earth ritual, make a note of it on your piece of paper, not forgetting where you are so you can retrace your steps later.

2. After you have engaged with your Earth symbol – and it may by now have flown away or moved on if it was an insect or animal – sit down and relax in a spot of your choice. If you're connecting with a flower or plant, then try to make your offering as near to it as you possibly can.
3. First dig your shallow hole and fill it with the wild stones. Now hold the malachite to your chest and repeat the following:

   'I am of Earth and so is this place
   With crystal green I make this space
   To hold the world within my hands
   And show my love for all Her lands.'

4. Place the malachite on top of the stones, then cover with earth, leaves, debris and more stones. Wind a length of string around the offering to seal your intention, and leave a marker stone on the surface.

The Air ritual

1. Air rituals tend to be more impromptu or impulsive. It may be that the weather changes before

your eyes, either improving or worsening, and you suddenly decide in that moment to act. You might look up by chance and see a cloud that resembles a face, or spot the sun dancing through the canopy of leaves overhead, or catch a glimpse of the moon in daylight. Whatever sparks off your Air ritual, make a note of it, not forgetting where you are so you can retrace your steps later.

2. Once you have established what it is that has made you feel a sense of the element Air, relax, sit down and focus on that moment. By now, the cloud formation may have changed, the atmosphere might feel slightly different, or the sun may have gone behind the clouds. It doesn't matter, because you engaged in that moment and know it for what it is and was, and recognised that it gave you meaning in life.
3. Take the citrine between your hands and hold it close to your belly as you say:

   'Take now this citrine, now this twine
   To bind my soul to earth's incline
   Where north is south and east is west
   And sun and moon reveal my quest.'

4. Dig a shallow hole and place the selection of polished stones into it, followed by the citrine. Cover with earth, leaves or weeds, and wind a piece of twine around the shrine to seal your intention. Leave a marker as usual.

The Water ritual

1. If you are lucky enough to live beside a spiritual monument or natural sacred source, then do visit it on this journey. But if you can't, don't worry, because you can create your own sacred site as you go along your way. When you come to a place that seems to embrace, welcome and engage with you, as you engage with it, then this may be your perfect spiritual site. It could be an empty beach, a grassy bank, a field of poppies, an old churchyard or a standing stone. Wherever it is and whatever is there, you will know this place when you find it, because it will radiate a sense of magic in itself; it will be a soulful place where it feels as if you could enter another world.
2. Build yourself a shrine by heaping up a pile of wild stones in the most hidden, secret place you can find – perhaps behind a bush or a rock, or in a tree hollow.
3. Sit down, relax and focus on your sacred site. Hold the amethyst between your hands, close to your heart chakra, as you say:

   'In this place is magic made
   A sacred site for every day
   Where soul and spirit dance in time
   Through portals to this special shrine.'

4. Dig a small hole beside the shrine and place the amethyst in it. Cover it with earth, leaves or

stones. Encircle the shrine with a piece of twine, and thank Mother Earth for finding you a place upon the planet where you can engage with the magic of the universe.

The Spirit ritual

1. By the time you have fulfilled all four element rituals, you may be near the end of your journey. But there's one final thing you need to do to find a true connection to nature.

   First, you will need to find a meaningful spot to finish your ritual pathway. You may be standing on a hill and watching the sunset, or delighting in the buzzing of bees, or reflecting on how you've achieved the first four magical rituals. It may well be the moment you decide to turn around and return home. As before, it's up to you to identify the spot that feels right.
2. For the Spirit ritual, there is no burial. You are just going to focus on your crystal. Hold the piece of clear quartz high above your head and look up to the sky. As you do so, say:

   'Where cows do moo
   And doves do coo
   This is the place to wake my soul;
   Where magic sings
   And birds take wing
   This is the place for spirit's gold.'

3. Now turn to face the east and repeat the verse, then do the same facing south, then west, then north.
4. With the ritual complete, put your quartz back in your bag. Before you start to head home, say:

'Light shone into my darkness today
A test, a nudge, a touch, it was the same
As if a dragonfly had come then gone away.
But more it was as if I knew
At last the path was open, free and true,
And if I changed direction, well no such loss
Just turn again to take the night to dusk.'

This affirms to the universe that you have truly connected and engaged with nature.

Retracing your steps

It's likely that you will want to revisit this trail and experience the magical unity you discovered, or return to your own sacred shrine and experience the invisible doors opening to universal energy once again. You can do this whenever you like. When you return to these special places, you may experience new qualities and feelings too.

Always carry your clear quartz with you. If you marked the spots well and made notes about where you buried the other crystals, you will be able to find the exact places. If things have been disturbed or aren't as you left them, it doesn't matter. This is nature: it changes, things move. If, by chance, one of your crystals is visible, take it home and treasure it – for, in a way, it's saying, 'Look, I am here to be with you, your journey is complete.'

PART FOUR

Crystal Protection and Healing

Since ancient times, crystals have featured in all forms of healing. They were used in elixirs and remedies for physical ailments, and some stones were worn to combat disease or protect from evil forces. They were turned to as a source of spiritual support and used to promote enlightenment.

A thirteenth-century magic book of talismans and amulets shows that a garnet ring engraved with a lion was thought to guard the wearer against all illnesses and protect during travelling. The ancient Egyptians used lapis lazuli to cure wealthy women of 'hysteria', while the less fortunate were given elixirs of malachite. Green stones were popular cures for eye disease in the medieval period, while yellow stones were used to cure jaundice and liver diseases, and red ones were used to calm inflammation, soothe aggression and heal cuts and scrapes. In Renaissance Italy, diamonds were believed to be antidotes for poison, and it was said they would turn dark in the presence of anything toxic, including evil intentions. In a thirteen-century Kashmir medical text, one physician describes how an elixir of rubies makes the perfect remedy for flatulence!

Native American healers used quartz to examine their patients, literally rubbing or rolling the crystal across the body to remove imbalances and restore harmony.

They also used the stones to pinpoint disease hotspots by observing the reaction of the skin as the quartz moved across it. However, it was believed the individual was healed by a spirit within the stone, not by the stone itself.

Contemporary crystal healing is informed by a synthesis of different practices and beliefs, such as Chinese acupuncture, Hindu anatomical wisdom and the Sanskrit system of chakras, as well as colour therapy and crystal vibrations. So why not explore some of the simple and safe (but still beneficial) qualities of your friendly stones and discover their ability to open you up to universal healing energy for the good of your mind, body and spirit?

Chapter 8

Practices for Protection and Healing

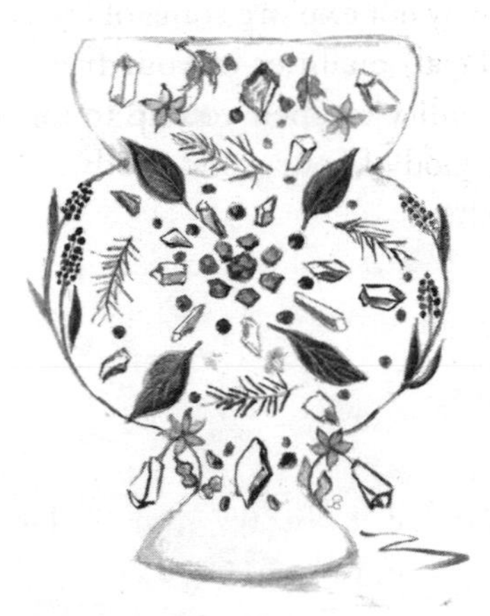

One of the simplest ways to use crystals for spiritual and physical protection is to carry them on your person, or wear them as jewellery, but you can also use them to protect your living space. Your home is a sanctuary, a space where you can safely reflect on past events and make plans for your future. To improve your spiritual connection, offer protection and boost your overall well-being, this chapter includes earth acupuncture and crystal grids to protect the home, as well as to promote self-awareness, serenity and empowerment. By working with crystals in these ways, you can protect and balance your home, your relationships with friends and family, you romantic partnerships and your work environment.

Negative energy

Before you begin any protection work, there are two forms of negative energy you need to understand.

Geopathic stress

This is the unwanted and usually negative effects of the Earth's environment on our well-being, including:

- polluted, stagnant or fast-flowing underground water courses
- diverted unnatural water courses that have been artificially manipulated
- electromagnetic trauma resulting from changes in the natural landscape
- 'sick' building syndrome, where you experience symptoms of ill health that are directly related to the time you've spent in a particular building
- techno-pathologies, such as radon accumulation and electric power lines
- effects of geomagnetic grids and unstable crossing points of ley lines or meridians

Geo-psychic stress

This is when the etheric or spiritual web of the Earth is traumatised by the presence of negative energy, such as:

- emotionally charged atmosphere created by spiritual entities
- traces of 'bad' energy left by previous occupants
- negative spirit energy left after traumatic events, such as accidents, deaths or war
- negative or highly disturbing earth meridians and ley lines that have been interfered with by man-made structures

Earth acupuncture and crystal grids

This practice of pinning, placing or burying crystals in the ground follows the same basic rules as the ancient Chinese art of acupuncture of the body, but here you are aligning to the invisible meridians and compass directions of the earth. For example, if you want to protect your home from negative energy, whether that's geopathic stress or unwanted psychic energy from people outside, you can lay an arrangement of crystals completely surrounding your property. (If this seems impractical, you can build a symbolic 'moat' around your home by creating a miniature outdoor grid.)

Crystal grids are powerful tools to use when you want to manifest your desires, goals and intentions. When you use a grid, the combined power of the stones you've chosen reinforces the beneficial energies of each individual crystal, so the strength of the grid is a bit like a team effort. The grids usually represent symbolic or sacred shapes, such as a pentagram, the flower of life or a mandala, establishing a strong bond to the universal matrix.

When constructing a grid, you need to make sure you have a flat surface to work on. You may want to use a board, or a black cloth placed on a table.

Ready-made grids

You can buy ready-made grid templates and patterns online, from geometric shapes and flamboyant mandalas, to simple ones with markers of where to place a few specific crystals. Look out for grids that may help you to achieve your goals and awaken your magical self.

Tip

To boost and amplify the power of your crystal grids, place your three power stones (see page 58) alongside the grid as you plot it out.

Crystal Acupuncture Grid to Protect the Home

Place this grid in a garden, in a flower pot beside your front door, or in an outside sanctuary you have created for spiritual or natural magic work. Choose somewhere where you can leave it and it won't be disturbed. It would be most beneficial if you can totally surround your home with the grid, but as this is usually impractical, a miniature or replica of the grid will work its magic too. The grid you'll create is aligned to the twelve zodiac signs, to encourage the perfect harmonious influence of the four astrological elements in which you will find wholeness.

You will need:

12 pieces of black tourmaline or black obsidian
a piece of clear quartz
12 sandalwood or cedarwood incense sticks

1. First, work out what size you intend to make this grid. If you would like to encircle your house and bury the crystals, you will obviously have to space them out over quite a large area, but creating this grid on a smaller scale in a sacred space outside, with the symbolic inclusion of yourself at the centre (represented by the clear quartz crystal) will provide the same influence and protection as it would if you managed to surround your home. It's just that fully encircling your home and burying

the crystals is more interactive and reinforces your innate connection to the earth itself.

2. The key here is to mimic the positioning of an astrological chart, where the signs of the zodiac start on the left side of a circle and revolve anti-clockwise. Take your first black crystal and place it on the westernmost point of your circle, and then, working anti-clockwise, arrange the remaining eleven crystals in a circle, spacing them out equally. If you are burying them in the ground around your home, push the sharp end of the crystal in first, then cover it up with soil and place a marker on top to remind you where it is. (The reason for burying them is to literally 'fix' or pin the energy of the crystal into the ground.)
3. Place the clear quartz in the centre of the circle (or in a central position in the interior of your home if burying the stones around its exterior), then light the twelve incense sticks and place one next to each black stone. Now say the following affirmation to seal your petition for protection and security:

   'For all who come and go from this home, for all who pass through, be safe and well
   This circle of stones will protect us all and keep us secure.
   Thank you, crystals, for your magical reward.'

4. Leave the grid in place. This is why, if you've made a miniature version, it's important to place

it somewhere where it won't be disturbed all year round. If you have to remove it, replace it when you can and repeat the above ritual. If you've made a large grid of crystals buried around the home, then there is little you have to do except remember to not dig up the crystals by accident when gardening!

Protective grid for home interior

This grid is left inside the home to protect all who live within.

You will need:

5 pieces of black tourmaline or black obsidian
8 pieces of clear quartz
a white candle

1. Place one black stone at the centre of your grid, then position the remaining four around it, spacing them out equally. Arrange the clear quartz crystals in a circle around the black stones.
2. Light the candle to consecrate the grid, and say:

'This light of crystals brings to my home and family, all the goodness and well-being within, to protect and nurture us.'

3. Touch each of the crystals and repeat the above affirmation each time to seal your intention for protective influence. Blow out the candle to end the ritual. Leave the grid in place all year round. If you need to remove the grid, simply replace it whenever you feel it is needed by repeating the ritual above.

Grid for Self-Awareness and Serene Communication

This grid amplifies self-awareness and the ability to communicate with understanding and acceptance.

You will need:

a piece of clear quartz to activate the grid
6 pieces of hematite
3 pieces of green aventurine
3 pieces of moonstone
6 pieces of lapis lazuli
4 pieces of peridot
a white candle

1. Place the clear quartz at the centre of your grid. Arrange the pieces of hematite in a circle around it, spacing them out evenly, then form a second circle around that made up of alternating pieces of green aventurine and moonstone. Next create

a star that encloses your circles using the six pieces of lapis lazuli, with one stone at each point of the star, and finally place the four pieces of peridot so that they form a square around your six-pointed star.

2. To consecrate the grid, light the white candle and repeat the following as you touch each crystal in turn:

   'Thank you, my friend, for enlightenment,
   clarity and self-assurance.'

3. Once you have finished, blow out the candle and leave the grid in place for at least one lunar cycle to reinforce all forms of communication and improve your awareness of your true desires. Recreate your grid whenever you feel that you're not getting your message across, or you find it hard to accept the reality of a situation.

Grid for Holistic Healing

This grid energises you and balances your general well-being.

You will need:

a piece of emerald
a piece of amethyst

a piece of obsidian
a piece of red carnelian
a piece of rose quartz
a piece of blue kyanite
a terminated clear quartz crystal to
activate the grid

1. Place the emerald at the centre of the grid, then use the other stones to create a five-pointed star around it, with the amethyst to the north-east, the obsidian to the south-east, the red carnelian to the south-west, the rose quartz to the north-west and the blue kyanite to the north.
2. Take up the terminated quartz and touch each stone with it to activate the stone's energy, then place the quartz to the south of the grid. Now touch each stone with your finger so that you may connect with their energy. As you do so, say:

'With healing powers of these six stones
I now can face the night alone
In harmony I find my way
To stand with strength for every day.'

3. Leave the grid in place for at least one lunar cycle to activate its beneficial holistic healing energy. Whenever you feel out of balance, repeat this grid.

Grid to Attract Romantic Relationships

When you are looking for love or hoping to attract someone new into your life, this spiral grid will amplify your intention. Not only will it empower you with charisma, but it will stir the universal energy into finding the right person for you.

You will need:

a piece of paper and a pen
12 pieces of rose quartz
12 pieces of rhodochrosite
a terminated clear quartz crystal

1. On the evening of a new crescent moon, write down your intention, making it very clear exactly what kind of person and relationship you are wishing for, for example: 'I want to attract someone who shares the same beliefs/interests/ambitions/desires and is kind/gentle/fun/loving.' Vocalise or visualise your intention as you fold up your piece of paper until it is not much bigger than one of your crystals. Place it on a flat surface to mark the centre of the grid.
2. Next, create a spiral pattern with your stones, working in a clockwise direction. Begin by placing the first stone on top of your piece of paper, then create your spiral outwards from there, alternating between rose quartz and rhodochrosite until you

have placed all twenty-four stones.

3. Activate the grid by touching each stone in turn with the quartz crystal. As you do so, say:

   'With these crystals my heart is bound
   This spiral web will make me found
   By someone right for my intentions
   Who finds me here with all attention.'

4. Leave your spiral until the full moon to maximise its power and attract someone new into your life.

Grid to Promote Sense of Achievement

You may long to change your career, make more money, achieve a long-term goal, or perhaps you want to feel successful and empowered. Whatever your goal, this grid will boost your ability to bring success into your life.

You will need:

a large image of an oak tree
9 citrine crystals
3 black tourmaline crystals

1. On the night of a waxing moon, place your image on a flat surface where it won't be disturbed for at least one lunar cycle. Place your stones beside the

image and then focus on your desire to be successful or feel a sense of achievement. As you do so, say:

'By stepping stones I make my way
A journey forth to bring me fame
With citrine gold or blackest stone
Success is mine for all winds blown.'

2. Now, one by one, place the citrine pieces in three parallel lines across your image. Finally, form a triangle around the citrine and oak tree with the black tourmaline pieces and say:

   'With oak tree blessed my will is done
   And all that's due me will be won.'

3. Leave until the full moon to promote achievement, self-belief, confidence and success.

Chapter 9

Chakras and Sacred Body Work

Chakras

As mentioned in the first chapter, the chakras are likened to epicentres of invisible energy that are believed to flow around and through the body. If any of the chakras are overactive or if their energies are blocked, you may find you have negative thoughts or become physically tired or stressed.

By wearing, carrying or using the corresponding

gemstone for each chakra, you can balance and restore your energy levels, improve your overall well-being, and bring harmony to your mind, body and spirit. Placing an appropriate crystal on a specific chakra will reinforce that chakra's energy and promote healing and balance. Each chakra has affinities with a specific colour, so by choosing crystals of the relevant colour, you can maximise that chakra's healing influence.

Here are the seven main chakras and their beneficial healing colours and crystals.

The crown chakra

Position
Top of the skull.

Colour
Violet/purple.

Crystals
Amethyst, labradorite, blue sapphire, clear quartz.

Keyword
Cosmic connection.

The crown chakra is a channel for the main flow of universal energy. It energises the whole chakra system, and is the centre for true spirituality. When this chakra is balanced, we can access the gift of cosmic consciousness, which can flow freely into us, bringing wisdom and enlightenment. When this chakra is unbalanced, you may experience a feeling of frustration, an uneasy sensitivity to the world around you, or a sense of meaninglessness about everything. Balancing the energy in this chakra gives you the ability to open up to cosmic wisdom and connect to the light of the universe that flows through all things, and restoring your *joie de vivre*.

If your crown chakra needs boosting or balancing

Close your eyes and simply imagine a pure white light shining down from above into your crown chakra: it radiates all around you and through you, right down to your toes. It fills you with cosmic knowledge, connection and joy of self. Now open your eyes and gaze into a clear quartz crystal and see the interconnectedness of the light within you and the light within the crystal. Take this crystal with you wherever you go to stimulate your cosmic connection.

The third eye or brow chakra

Position

Centre of the forehead.

Colour

Indigo.

Crystals

Amethyst, azurite, fluorite, sodalite.

Keyword
Intuition.

Vibrating to colours ranging from purple to indigo, the third eye chakra is the channel for inspiration, imagination and psychic ability. When balanced, it promotes our ability to utilise our psychic awareness, develop our imagination and be creative. When this chakra is not balanced, you may be blind to the truth, non-assertive, afraid of success and indecisive. You may not have any psychic awareness, or trust your intuition, relying instead on what other people say to you or searching constantly for logical reasoning, not believing there is any other way to look at life.

If your third eye chakra needs restoring or balancing
Hold a piece of amethyst to the centre of your forehead for a few minutes while you imagine manifesting the thing you desire most in the world. See your success and visualise the word 'success' written on the amethyst. Come out of your visualisation and place the amethyst under your pillow for one lunar cycle. You will soon restore both your psychic powers and creative skills, trusting in your own inner voice and asserting your beliefs and desires.

The throat chakra

Position
Middle to lower part of throat.

Colour
Blue.

Crystals
Blue lace agate, aquamarine, lapis lazuli.

Keyword
Communication.

The throat chakra is the centre for thought, communication, music, speech and writing. By energising this chakra, you will improve your communication and negotiation skills. Keeping the throat chakra balanced means you can express yourself truthfully, and it also encourages the same from those around you. When it's restored and energised, this chakra enables successful transactions and helps you accept and appreciate others' differences. When it's out of balance, you may feel timid, not say much, resent others who speak freely, misunderstand peers, or find it difficult to express your thoughts.

If your throat chakra is blocked or needs restoring
Put a piece of lapis lazuli in front of a mirror, then gaze at your reflection and say, 'I am empowered and ready to speak as my true self.' Take the crystal and hold it to your throat while repeating the same words. Wear the lapis or carry it with you for more spontaneous and beneficial interactions and communication with others.

The heart chakra

Position
Centre breastbone.

Colour
Green.

Crystals
Green aventurine, green jade, emerald.

Keyword
Love.

The heart chakra is the centre of warm, loving feelings. Through the heart chakra, we have the ability to feel compassion and to experience the power of unconditional love. It also helps us to accept other people's faults and respect their differences. If the heart chakra is in balance, then the rest of our psyche usually flows well, too, as this chakra is the channel connecting the mind with the soul and body. When the heart chakra is balanced, you feel a sense of harmony, calm and self-confidence, and have the ability to fully appreciate good relationships. When this chakra is diminished, you may be afraid of revealing your feelings for fear of getting hurt, and you may begrudge others their good fortune, or judge them – and yourself – too quickly. You may remain cool and distant, and not give much away about yourself.

If your heart chakra is blocked or out of balance

To restore compassion, write on a piece of paper 'I love myself and the universe' and wrap it around a piece of emerald. Hide the stone in the most secret place in your home for a full moon cycle, then remove it and show your love for the stone by carrying it with you to restore love for yourself and for others.

The solar plexus chakra

Position

Midway between navel and ribs.

Colour

Yellow.

Crystals

Citrine, yellow aventurine, yellow tourmaline.

Keyword

Ego.

Relating to your ego's energy levels, this chakra is the seat of personal power. This is our solar centre, the powerhouse of our psyche that gives us a sense of our own personal character, our individuality and willpower. Maintaining a balanced solar plexus chakra aids self-confidence, self-esteem, motivation and purpose. If this chakra isn't shining like a true sun, then we may let others dominate us; we might feel afraid to express our personal opinion, or worry about what others will think about what we believe or say.

If your solar plexus chakra is blocked or needs restoring

To rediscover your individual self-expression or to amplify your voice if you feel you're not being heard, sit in a comfortable position and relax. Take a piece of citrine and hold it in your hands close to the solar plexus chakra. Close your eyes and imagine a sun shining forth from this chakra, connecting its light to the stone. Focus on this image for a few minutes, then take the citrine with you wherever you go to bring that inner spark to life and empower you with self-reliance, composure and determination.

The sacral chakra

Position

A hand's breadth below the navel.

Colour

Orange.

Crystals

Carnelian, tiger's eye, orange jasper.

Keywords

Emotions and sexuality.

The sacral chakra is concerned with our sex lives, creativity and emotional being. When we feel stressed or disturbed by others, this is the chakra that will need rebalancing and restoring, and crystals placed here will heal anxiety, release tension and revive our sense of pleasure, happiness and well-being. If this chakra is underactive, you'll have little confidence in your sexuality and fear getting close to anyone. You may have problems relating to other people and fear they just want you as a sexual object. There's a chance that you may get stressed by other people's demands and worry that you're not good enough.

If your sacral chakra is blocked or needs restoring

Place a piece of tiger's eye on a sunny windowsill or outside in the sun for twenty-four hours to charge it with solar and lunar energy. Keep the charged crystal close to your sacral chakra for another twenty-four hours to restore and energise your sensual side, boost your sex drive or relieve stress.

The base or root chakra

Position

Base of the spine.

Colour

Red.

Crystals
Bloodstone, ruby, garnet, red jasper.

Keyword
Grounded.

This chakra is concerned with being grounded and is the base energy through which we feel at one with the Earth and the universe. When this chakra is balanced, we know our place in the world; we understand what we need to do on our life journey, and how to develop or express our talents and our individuality. If you're feeling confused or distracted by too many problems, or finding it difficult to focus on what's really important, this is the chakra to rebalance. If you have a feeble base chakra, you might feel spaced out and not in touch with the world, threatened by other people, or unable to get any project under way, with a sense of never finishing what you start.

If your base chakra is blocked or needs restoring
Place a piece of bloodstone under your bed in line with this area of your body when you're lying down. Leave for one lunar cycle to energise and ground you, enable you to make important decisions, or help you to recognise what really matters to you in life.

Palm chakras

Position
Centre of the palm of hand.

Colour
Clear, white or iridescent.

Crystals
Clear quartz, selenite, moonstone, opal.

Keyword
Exchange.

These chakras are concerned with exchanging energy. Here we give and receive, offer and accept, and reach out and reap rewards. When these chakras are not in balance, we find it difficult to support others, and may put up defences to protect us from our fear of intimacy. However, when these energy centres are in balance, we feel in tune with nature and the universe and are able to accept every day as it comes – and we will find it easier to use crystals to empower us to connect us to the universal energy flow. Complete the ritual below.

Getting in touch with your palm chakras

You will need:

a white candle
2 pieces of clear quartz

1. Light the candle and place your two quartz crystals in front of it. Close your eyes for a moment with your hands outstretched on the table before you, palms facing up, as if to receive the flow of universal energy.
2. Now open your eyes and focus on the crystals. Imagine one of the crystals is resting in the palm of each hand. As soon as the crystal touches your skin, you will feel empowered and blessed.
3. Take one of the crystals in your right hand and let it lie in your open palm. Can you feel its warmth, its energy, its harmonious influence? Do the same with the other crystal in your left hand and experience the sensations in both palms as you hold them out in front of you towards the candle flame. Place the crystals in front of the candle again, and thank them for connecting you to the energy of the universe.
4. Your palm chakras are now activated, and you will find that the more you hold and touch crystals, the more you will feel empowered and connected to them and therefore to the universe.

Experiencing the Chakras

Before you use any crystals for chakra restoration, it's important to get in touch with all the chakra energy centres.

You will need:

a terminated clear quartz crystal

1. Find a quiet place. Sit on the ground, preferably cross-legged, and relax. Place the crystal between both hands and imagine your base chakra rooting you to the ground. Holding your crystal a few inches away from this area of your body, with the point directed away from you, close your eyes and feel its vibrational energy. Imagine the colour red as the crystal connects to your chakra.
2. After about a minute, move your crystal up to the sacral chakra area and do the same thing, this time imagining the qualities and colours associated with this chakra.
3. Do the same with all your chakras. When you reach the crown chakra, hold the crystal above your head and imagine the energy of the universe flowing through it and directly into your chakra.
4. Gently return your hands to your lap, still holding the crystal. Now imagine that you are sending the powerful energy from the crown chakra down to the base chakra, then allowing

it to flow back up again. Visualise this circuit of energy flowing through your body whenever you feel vulnerable. This will empower you, and help you to connect to the universal energy to help balance all chakras.

5. Now you need to close your chakras. Think of each chakra as an open book, and as you work from the crown chakra to the base chakra, close each one. And as you do so, repeat the following phrase:

'I have now closed the book of [name of chakra].'

Crystals for alternative self-care practices

Meditation, mindfulness, yoga and all kinds of alternative self-care practices can be complemented by and boosted with the inclusion of crystals. Crystals are not only our friends, they are also powerful symbols of our inner world and spiritual needs.

Here are seven specific crystals that will help you create harmony and balance in your life, to restore body, mind or spirit. You can incorporate them into your practices to promote peace, love, protection, self-acceptance and strength.

You can either invest in large statement crystals that can be displayed permanently in your practice space, or use tumbled stones or raw crystals placed in a special bowl or on a sacred cloth. Alternatively, you can align your crystals with your yoga mat or preferred meditation direction.

Clear quartz

As already discussed, terminated clear quartz crystals amplify the energy and intentions of all other stones, and this beautiful fragment of Mother Earth is well suited to meditation, helping to promote clarity of mind and inner peace, and deepening one's altered state of consciousness.

Amethyst

Meditating with amethyst promotes an intuitive connection to the universe and boosts the stone's powers of peace, stability, patience and inner strength. It helps purify the mind of negative thoughts. When placed near your yoga mat, amethyst will boost your physical strength and stamina.

Hematite

If you practise yoga and have problems with standing or balancing poses, hematite enhances concentration and focus, and promotes confidence and poise. This protective stone activates the root chakra to help you stay grounded in all forms of alternative practices.

Selenite

Selenite is associated with the moon and is the ultimate stone to use when you seek spiritual truth or need to find inner peace and harmony. Add selenite to your practice space when you want to channel purity and stillness, or to help clear the mind and enhance connection to your soul. It is best used between the new crescent moon and full moon to awaken your spiritual self, but if used in the dark of the moon phase, it can bring awareness of your deepest truth.

Labradorite

Enhancing all forms of psychic awareness, this stone is the perfect companion for alternative states of consciousness, such as astral projection (an out-of-body experience of one's soul travelling through the universe), telepathy, past-life work and for seeing the truth of who you are. It also promotes flexibility and balance, and so provides a gentle but positive boost for all forms of yoga, Pilates and other body work.

Azurite

This beautiful blue stone amplifies our connection to our psychic world, encouraging and opening up the pathway for enlightenment and the realisation that all is one. It clears confusion, relieves tension, and relaxes and calms the stresses of the mind. It can be used in any kind of spiritual practice to enhance total involvement in sacred wisdom.

Celestite

This ethereal blue stone enables us to feel a sense of belonging and appreciate that we are part of the universe and that we can connect to our souls. Celestite is useful for any kind of practice where we want to contact or draw on the power of spirit guides and angels, and can also help with out-of-body travel, clairvoyance and other psychic skills. When placed in your practice room, it will heighten your awareness of the energy that permeates all things, and will encourage you to trust in divine or sacred energy.

Meditation

Meditation and mindfulness allow us to free ourselves from the busy chattering of the mind and the world around us. While in a meditative state, we can – even momentarily – see the truth of ourselves, our inner wisdom and our connection to the universe. Crystals will help you to open up your mind, body and spirit, and free you from the distractions of the daily world.

There are two beneficial ways to meditate with crystals. One is by holding one special crystal to enhance its specific energies; the other is by surrounding your meditation space with a series of crystals to open your mind and protect your open state of being.

Holding a crystal

As you hold a crystal between both hands, or one in each hand if you prefer, you are developing a tangible and physical connection to the crystal. This means you and the crystal are linked as a circuit of exchanging energy. The crystal becomes a conduit, helping you to align to the earth, planetary and universal energies around you.

Surrounding yourself with crystals

Creating a crystal circle connects you to crystal energy without any need to physically touch the crystal. This is a personal preference: people prefer not to physically touch crystals as they meditate, as it can seem like an intrusion into their meditative state and may 'put them off' their pathway.

So if you prefer simply being surrounded by crystal energy, place one to the north of you, one to the south, one to the east and one to the west. Choose four crystals that enhance the kind of energy you are working with. Alternatively, you can select four different stones that add different energies to help balance out your practice.

Yoga and other body work

You can place specific crystals around your yoga mat, or use one large centrepiece positioned in the direction of your choice. A grid arrangement around the room can also work well to promote general well-being, and boost your ability to focus and align with the energy of your poses.

Small tumbled stones will work just as well as larger pieces, and the grid will remind you to focus on its power throughout your practice.

A SIMPLE GRID

You will need:

8 crystals of your choice
a large piece of clear quartz or your focus stone

1. Place one crystal to the north of you, one to the north-east, one to the east, one to the south-east, one to the south, one to the south-west, one to the west and one to the north-west. Place the clear quartz in the centre of the mat so you can focus on it while in a pose.
2. The crystal grid will protect and vitalise you, bringing you into harmony with your body work, while the quartz or focus stone will enable you to feel connected to your spiritual practice.

Other ways to incorporate crystals into your yoga practice

- Wear a crystal pendant or bracelet during your practice to empower you with its specific qualities.
- Carry a crystal in your yoga bag to charge your mat with its power. If you are practising at home, place your crystals along the edge

of your mat, then roll it up and leave it in place overnight so that it can be charged with crystal energy.

- Place one or more crystals on any or all of your chakras during *shavasana* (the completion of yoga practice when you lie on your back for several minutes). For general spiritual connection and healing, place on the crown and third eye chakras. If you feel you need to restore a specific chakra, use its associated crystal for a gentle healing session.

PART FIVE

Crystal Divination

So, what is divination? Well, in magic, it's about looking at life in a different way and using that knowledge to make your life what you want it to be. Divination is the transmission of information via signs, symbols and patterns that connect us to the underlying universal energy at any one moment in time, helping us to shape our future. In divination, every image, smile, rustling tree, falling star, intuitive moment or flash of insight is an important sign or symbol revealing invisible truths, because everything is interwoven in the great tapestry of the universe.

Divination comes from the Latin word *divinare*, meaning 'to be inspired by the gods'. Whether we believe the information is being revealed to us by the gods or the cosmos, when we work with the archetypal energy of symbolic associations and correspondences, we are opening ourselves up to the collective unconscious and the storehouse of universal knowledge that permeates all.

The art of divination opens you up to your intuitive awareness, and reveals inner truths about your past, future and present, all wrapped up in the moment that is now. It also brings conscious realisation that you have control over which pathway you chose to follow. It is you who must make the choices and take responsibility for your future based on this present moment.

Chapter 10

Oracles and Interpretations

As we've seen, the vibrational energy of a crystal is a powerful conduit for universal energy. We can place crystals in special layouts or grids to create magic symbols to attract specific desires (see part four) and augment intention by casting spells and performing rituals (see part three). In divination, we can take a crystal from a pouch and use it as an oracle, cast crystals on to a zodiac chart, or read the colours and shapes that crystals make under candlelight (see page 226). We'll start with the simplest way to divine with crystals: using them as oracles. First, you need to prepare yourself.

Wishful thinking and intention

Before you begin any divination work, you need to be sure you are also aware of your true intentions. It's important to remember to **read the moment that is being revealed to you, rather than reading into the crystals what you would like to happen.**

Symbols never lie. They mirror our current state of being, and therefore we must learn to trust in the moment when we reveal the oracle or outcome. If we do this, we can also trust in ourselves.

Practice for Focus and Seeing

This ritual will help you get in touch with your unconscious and open it up to the world of symbols and archetypes.

You will need:

a piece of clear quartz

1. Find a comfortable and private space. You may prefer to sit on the floor in a yoga pose with hands

rested on your knees, or at a table with your palms facing upwards. Whatever you choose, make sure you are in a relaxed and receptive state.

2. Close your eyes and pay close attention to your breathing. Count each breath as you breathe in and out until you reach twenty.
3. Now turn your focus to the outside world. What do you hear, if anything? Is there a distant buzz of traffic, an echo of chatter, a rustle of leaves or just the sound of silence?
4. Focus on seeing – not with your eyes, but with your deep insight and intuition. Can you intuit or imagine what is in the distance? You may know what is in your immediate environment, but can you see beyond, further into the distance, along a road that you have not yet travelled down? Can you see a place that is unknown to you physically, yet somehow feels deeply familiar?
5. After five minutes of this kind of reflection, open your eyes and gaze into the crystal. What do you see? Try to describe the image out loud. Is it a person, an idea, a spirit guide, a cloud, a shape, a fuzzy shadow? What you see is relevant, because your imagination connects visual information with your unconscious and processes it to give that image meaning. This is the pathway to the hidden messages the universe holds for you. This is the way intuition and imagination work together to bring you a deeper understanding of divination.
6. Come out of your focused state and place your

crystal in a safe place, then go about your day. Practise this ritual at times when you struggle to focus, or when you have lost your intuitive way of looking at the world, and it will restore your ability to 'see' from a different perspective.

Preparing for readings

After cleansing your crystals (page 28) and gathering your tools, it doesn't matter too much where you perform your readings. The most important thing is that you choose a space that feels comfortable and appropriate to you. The more at home you feel in your surroundings, the more you are able to connect to that inner numinous world. Whether you're a nomadic type who spontaneously casts crystals on the go, or someone who likes a specific ritual and space, it is for you to make that choice.

Two special stones for divination

There are two stones that can help to put you in the right mindset for divination: phantom quartz crystal and onyx.

When choosing your phantom quartz, opt for a piece that has a lovely pattern and a blend of colours, as this will help to illuminate you with knowledge. Make sure you place the crystal to your right during your divination practice, as phantom quartz is associated with clarity and truth, and the right side of your brain is associated with intuition and imagination.

Onyx is an integral stone as it helps to prevent you from projecting your own desires or thoughts on to the reading. Place this on your left, so that the left side of your brain's psychological hang-ups, defences and projections are absorbed by the stone.

Choosing your other stones

Next, you need to decide which stones you want to use for divination. A good balance of colours and meanings is recommended here. The following list provides a selection of the most common crystals and their keywords when specifically used for divination. Choose as many as you like, but start with at least ten. The associated keyword can be used as a quick guide to interpretation, but there are more detailed oracle meanings on pages 215–222.

Amber: joy
Amethyst: truth
Aquamarine: intuition
Black tourmaline: security
Bloodstone: determination
Blue lace agate: clarity
Celestite: self-awareness
Citrine: optimism
Clear quartz: activation

Emerald: shrewdness
Fire agate: reflection
Garnet: willpower
Green aventurine: advice
Green tourmaline: prosperity
Jade: reward
Kyanite: trust
Lapis lazuli: revelation
Magnetite: tenacity
Malachite: opportunity
Moonstone: insight
Morganite: romance
Obsidian: self-reliance
Onyx: goodness
Opal: foresight
Orange calcite: focus
Peridot: chance
Pink sapphire: emotions
Red carnelian: challenge
Red jasper: success
Rhodochrosite: acceptance
Rhodolite: desire
Rhodonite: passion
Rose quartz: harmony
Ruby: achievement
Sapphire: wisdom
Selenite: compassion
Smoky quartz: breakthrough
Sodalite: communication
Sunstone: opportunity

Tiger's eye: success
Turquoise: solution
White topaz: peace
Yellow fluorite: priorities
Yellow topaz: decisiveness

Crystal of the Day Oracle

One of the simplest forms of crystal divination, and the best way to learn how to interpret crystals, is to randomly choose one for the day. This is particularly useful if you have a significant event ahead, like a date, a career opportunity or an exam, and you are in need of some targeted insight.

You will need:

a selection of different-coloured rough or polished/tumbled crystals (about 10 will probably be enough to start with, but as you get more used to reading crystals, you can add more)
an opaque pouch

The reading

1. Place the crystals in the pouch and then gently shake it for around ten seconds. As you do so, focus on your intentions for the day or the specific event

in question. A positive intention usually brings a positive outcome, because it shows you believe in yourself and are in control of your life rather than being controlled by external influences.

2. Close your eyes, open the pouch and take the first stone you touch – no cheating! Pull the stone from the pouch and hold it in your hand for a few seconds before you open your eyes.

Interpretation

1. Now gaze at your crystal. You may instinctively know what it's trying to tell you, but you need to give voice to your intuition to create a meaningful story. If it's not immediately clear what the crystal signifies, then you can use the list below to help intuit its meaning. Remember, these interpretations are not set in stone (excuse the pun) so feel free to associate or relate these ideas with things that have relevance to your personal life or future intentions.
2. If, for example, the stone you pull from the pouch is a piece of black tourmaline, you might look up the common interpretation of the stone – security. Keep this in mind throughout the day and try to observe and notice things that may not have caught your eye before. Consciously look for signs, symbols or experiences that relate to the crystal's basic meaning. This is also an empowering way to get to know the crystal's intentions, sacred use, and purpose in your life.

Interpreting crystal oracles

Here are some more in-depth interpretations of different crystal oracles. You can also use these as a basis for other forms of crystal divination.

Blue and purple stones

These are connected to our feeling world, emotions and moods.

Amethyst

An emotional challenge lies ahead, or self-discipline is needed. Focus on practical goals and don't let your imagination run away with you.

Aquamarine

Use your intuition to read between the lines and do not let others deceive you. The more objective you are, the more enjoyable your day will be.

Blue lace agate

It is time to be clear about your true desires.

Celestite

A meaningful coincidence will occur: you may enjoy a lucky break, or experience a day when you feel spiritually uplifted and self-aware.

Kyanite
It is time to speak up and make it clear what's on your mind, but only to someone who you can trust.

Lapis lazuli
A revelatory moment will give you hope.

Sapphire
Some wise advice from someone important will bring you peace of mind.

Sodalite
Expect good communication and news that will enable you to resolve a problem.

Red stones
These are connected to action, desire, purpose and motivation.

Bloodstone
Determination will score you points; you can succeed against all the odds. Courage is needed to make your mark.

Fire agate
A desire may be fulfilled, but take care you don't rush into a commitment without thinking it through. Think before acting.

GARNET

Willpower is needed, or a strong attachment formed. Inspirational or creative ideas come to you, but you will need to stay grounded to make them work.

RED CARNELIAN

Endure any challenge you face, and you will be rewarded. Go with the flow and enjoy the harmonious energy around you.

RED JASPER

This signifies success, results and achievement, or the ability to take a stagnant idea and bring it to fruition.

RUBY

You will experience a potent encounter, or a commitment can be made. Self-confidence and expressing your desires will bring you a sense of achievement.

SUNSTONE

Opportunity knocks – don't miss it. Seize the day and make a grounded decision.

Pink stones

These are connected to love, romance and harmony.

PINK SAPPHIRE

This signifies emotional honesty between you and a loved one. You will enjoy harmony and overcome psychological fears.

Pink tourmaline
Listen to your heart and speak up. Romance will blossom, or you will feel ready to start a new relationship.

Rhodochrosite
Accept and care for yourself and cast off your old defences. New romance or close friendship will come to you from someone you already know.

Rhodolite
Another will desire you, but be cautious if you reciprocate. Your creative ideas can be put to the test, but don't give them away freely.

Rhodonite
A passionate exchange is made. Questions will arise, such as who do you really want to be with, and do you really know who you are?

Rose quartz
Signifies harmony between you and a partner or friend. An encounter will bring romantic longings. Forgiveness will heal a rift.

Clear, white and iridescent stones
These are connected to truth and illumination.

Clear quartz
A time when you realise what it is you desire and why. Success will come your way if you keep a clear head and stay sure of your goal.

Moonstone
New beginnings or spiritual clarity beckon. You will have a flash of insight and the ability to see what you really want in life.

Opal
Positive news or a chance encounter comes your way at last. You can now step across the threshold and find a new way to live better.

Selenite
Peaceful feelings: harmony abounds. Your compassionate nature will be put to the test.

White topaz
Peace of mind; an epiphany; a wake-up call to the truth of who you are and where you are going.

Yellow and orange stones
These are connected to communication, the mind and intention.

Amber
Close friends or loved ones bring unexpected good news. A joyful atmosphere will give you the feel-good factor.

Citrine

An optimistic time for making your objectives clear to someone. Rewards are coming your way.

Orange calcite

Pure intellectual power and focus will bring you great contacts or useful information.

Yellow fluorite

You will find something you thought you had lost. Quick thinking is needed to get your priorities right.

Yellow topaz

A decision needs to be made. Use logic and be realistic about what you can achieve, and you will attain your goal.

Green stones

These are connected to the material world, wisdom and power.

Emerald

You will be wise enough to not let someone's negative comments get to you.

Green aventurine

Information or advice from a powerful friend or contact will lead the way to a better future.

Green tourmaline

You attract the attention of someone who can help you make a profitable decision. Creative ideas will give you the prosperity you seek.

Jade

Financial rewards can be achieved – if you are generous towards others, too.

Malachite

Look out for a financial opportunity. Material resourcefulness is needed.

Peridot

Take a chance – a new opportunity could help you to achieve more than you imagine possible.

Turquoise

A solution is found to a difficult problem, but you will need to travel further than you thought to resolve it.

Brown and black stones

These are connected to security, protection and determined effort.

Black tourmaline

The air clears and you can see the way forward. Ground your ideas and you will find the security you seek.

MAGNETITE
Endurance and tenacity are needed to move forward. If you knuckle down, you will soon attract prosperity.

OBSIDIAN
Stand up for your beliefs and desires, and don't let anyone put you off track. Self-confidence is needed to make a material gain.

ONYX
Good fortune, happiness and reward await you.

SMOKY QUARTZ
The truth will be revealed, and you will begin to make a breakthrough on an emotional issue.

TIGER'S EYE
Stay determined and focused, and you will succeed in any money-making or material venture.

Simple crystal readings

Crystal reading is a magical way to understand who you are at any moment in time, and what issues you are experiencing that may need to be resolved in the future.

Now that you've tried some simple crystal oracle work, you can start to read crystal spreads to give you a bigger picture of what's going on in your life. Like reading tarot cards, reading crystals is simply about tuning in to your intuitive mind, opening yourself up to the story behind the crystal in front of you, and relating it to your question or the intention, as well as paying attention to the placement of the crystal on the table and what that implies.

Always keep your reading stones separate from all other crystals, as their energy is then specifically geared towards divining.

Try these simple crystal spreads, and once you've got used to interpreting the stones, you can make up your own too, gearing them to specific questions and issues you might want to explore.

'Now', 'then', 'will be' spread

This spread clarifies any current situation or question that needs resolving, allowing you to make a decision about the near future based on that knowledge.

You will need:

a pouch of at least 10 stones in different colours

1. Close your eyes, relax and focus on any issue or question. Gently shake your pouch of crystals, then take out the first crystal you touch. This is the 'now' crystal. Place it directly in front of you.
2. Shake the pouch gently again, then reach in and

place the second crystal to the left of the first. This is the 'then' crystal.

3. Repeat the above and place the third crystal to the right of the first. This is the 'will be' crystal.
4. To help you interpret your layout, refer to the meanings as given on pages 215–222.

   For example, let's say you choose citrine as the 'now' crystal, red carnelian as the 'then' crystal, and amber as the 'will be' crystal.

   The following interpretations are based on keywords and traditional meanings, combined with a personal story. Always remember to relate the reading to the person who is the seeker of answers (for now, that's you), and to any specific question, if there is one. You are telling yourself about *you*; you are telling your story.

- **'Now' crystal – citrine:** *Right now, communication and the ability to talk through a problem is essential for me.*
- **'Then' crystal – red carnelian:** *Someone pushed me for answers, and I felt pressured, but I'm ready now to say what I believe.*
- **'Will be' crystal – amber:** *A joyful or unexpected encounter will prove rewarding and change my destiny.*

Shadow and Fortune Spread

This spread will reveal what it is you're really searching for in life right now, and show you the influences that may be helpful – or not so helpful – as you make your way forwards.

You will need:

a pouch of at least 10 stones in different colours

1. Close your eyes and focus on an issue or question. When you're ready, remove five crystals from the pouch, one at a time. Lay them out so that they form the points of a compass, with the first to the north, the second to the south, the third to the east and the fourth to the west. Place the fifth stone in the middle.
2. The first (north) crystal is the crystal of shadows, representing unhelpful influences, people or blockages. The second (south) crystal is the crystal of dreams, representing what your current desires and needs are. The third (east) crystal is the crystal of illusions, representing things that are unrealistic or unattainable right now. The fourth (west) crystal is the crystal of benefits, representing helpful influences. The fifth (centre) crystal is the crystal of fortune, which represents the outcome.

Romantic relationship test spread

This spread is useful to clarify your intentions and desires in a romantic relationship. It will give you a clue as to what your partner or any new admirer is feeling too.

You will need:

a pouch of at least 12 stones in different colours

1. Close your eyes, gently shake your pouch of crystals, and focus on the relationship in question.
2. This spread is made up of seven crystals. You want to form two vertical lines of three crystals each, placing the first crystal on the left, the second to the right of it, and so on. Your seventh crystal is your outcome crystal: place this beneath both your lines at the midway point.
3. The crystals signify:
    1. Your intentions for the relationship
    2. Your partner's intentions
    3. Your doubts or concerns
    4. Your partner's doubts or concerns
    5. How you feel about your partner
    6. How your partner feels about you
    7. The outcome

SACRED STONE ORACLE

Here is another magical way to cast and interpret crystal oracles. It is based on the ancient Greek myth of three prophetic nymphs known as the Thriae. You do need to be very open and receptive visually for this practice, and must be willing to try it a few times if it doesn't come together on your first attempt.

The Thriae divined the future by casting stones into a clear stream on the night of a full moon. They interpreted the colours and patterns made by the crystals created in the water's reflections. In the popular folklore of the time, it was believed that if you came across the Thriae, you could ask them to tell you your future, but only if you offered them a sapphire to prove you were worthy of their divine advice.

The Thriae's names reflected their oracular replies. Melena, meaning 'black', is associated with the stone of darkness and the past; Kleodora, meaning 'gift', is associated with the stone of gifting and the present; and Daphnis, meaning 'laurel', is associated with the stone of light and the future.

You will need:

5 white candles
a large mirror
a large glass bowl of water
2 pieces of clear quartz
2 blue stones

2 red stones
2 yellow or orange stones
2 black or brown stones
2 green stones
a pouch

1. On the night of a full moon, place the five candles in a line in front of your mirror, positioning them with enough distance from the mirror to create a powerful reflected light.
2. Place the bowl of water between you and the candles, then light the candles. Put all the crystals in the pouch.
3. Now recite the following verse:

   'Melena's past shows me the way
   Kleodora's gift, my purpose today
   Daphnis' light will shine for me
   And show me what will be must be.'

4. Shake the pouch gently for a minute while you focus on your intention, issue or question, then tip the crystals gently into the bowl of water.
5. Now place your hand into the water and gently stir it round. As you do so, gaze into the bowl and search for any colours you might see reflected by the candlelight and the crystals themselves.
6. Continuing to swirl your fingers gently around in the water, now look at the reflection of the bowl in the mirror and examine the colours you

can see. The source of colours doesn't matter – it could be the crystal glow itself, the dancing lights in the water, the mirror, the glass bowl or the candle flames. As soon as you notice one colour standing out from the rest, stop swirling your hand.

7. Remove the crystal that is the closest in colour to the reflections you saw and place it to the left of the bowl. This is Melena's 'stone of darkness': the past.
8. Perform the same action as above, and take out the next stone. Place it to the right of the bowl. This is Daphnis' 'stone of light': the future.
9. Repeat the ritual again and take out the last stone. Place it before you, between the two other stones. This is Kleodora's 'stone of the gift': the present.
10. Use the 'Interpreting crystal oracles' guide on pages 215–222 as a basis for your own personal interpretation of the stones you have selected.

Chapter 11

Zodiac Crystal Divination

Before you start to work with crystals and zodiac divination, it's important to understand a bit about the astrological birth chart.

The horoscope, or birth chart, is made up of twelve zodiac signs, showing the position of planets and the angles or 'aspects' between those planets. It is also divided into twelve 'houses', which are determined by where in the world, and at what time of the day, you were born. There are various other components that make up the birth chart, but for the purposes of divination, we are just going to work with the houses.

The houses traditionally tell you the areas of life where the energies of the planets and zodiac signs will manifest. For example, if your sun is in Aries in your tenth house, you'll find that your Aries sun-sign motivation will bring you success or esteemed public or business profile. This is because the sun in Aries refers to dynamism, while the tenth house refers to career, ambition and visibility. Similarly, if you were born with the sun in Aries in the fourth house, then your pioneering spirit would be best channelled into your home life and family, as these are fourth-house qualities.

By casting the crystals associated with the signs and planets of the zodiac across a divinatory board, you will discover which areas of your life require attention now, or in the near future.

The placement of the fallen crystals (the way they are grouped) and their own divinatory properties are all read in tandem. This is obviously more complex than a simple crystal reading, but with practice, it will develop your intuitive powers and connect you closer to the crystal energy around you. With time, you will be able to read the crystal patterns and layouts without having to consciously analyse everything.

Crystals in the houses of the zodiac

The First House of the Self

Ruling energy: Aries

KEYWORDS

Physical appearance, first impressions, the way you perceive the world, individuality.

MEANING

Think about what your issue or question says about you; you may find the answer within you, not without.

COLOUR

Red crystals indicate you need to act; blue that you need to think before you act; yellow that you need to communicate your ego needs; green, black and brown, that you need some personal advice on the subject in question.

The Second House of Possessions

Ruling energy: Taurus

KEYWORDS

Possessions, values, money, stability.

MEANING

Relating your question or issue to your financial attitude may help to decide what choices are available to you; or perhaps your values are the key to resolving your problem.

Colour

Clear, red or green crystals can suggest financial changes need to be made, while yellow and clouded white indicate more honesty is needed.

The Third House of Communication
Ruling energy: Gemini

Keywords

Exchange, communication, ideas, short trips.

Meaning

Crystals here point to the way you communicate, or suggest you are in need of counsel from your friends or family. A journey may help resolve the issue.

Colour

Clear, yellow or red crystals indicate you need to be precise in any communication; blue that you need to trust your intuition and not be so logically minded; green or brown suggest that you need to ground your ideas.

The Fourth House of Home and Family
Ruling energy: Cancer

Keywords

Home, family, feelings, caring.

Meaning

Relate your question to your home and family life, which may be causing you some feelings of insecurity; prioritise and care about yourself first.

Colour

Green and blue crystals suggest you need to be less dependent on others, while clear or red crystals indicate you will soon be surrounded by those who care for you.

The Fifth House of Pleasure

Ruling energy: Leo

Keywords

Romance, creativity, pleasure.

Meaning

Crystals that fall here indicate that you need to lighten up and enjoy life more, or that new romance is winging its way towards you.

Colour

Pink or red crystals provide particularly potent energy when landing in this house; clear, yellow or blue crystals suggest creative opportunities on the horizon.

The Sixth House of Health and Work

Ruling energy: Virgo

Keywords

Work, efficiency, order, skill, healing.

Meaning

Any work issues will become more apparent if crystals fall here, and it may indicate that you're not focusing enough on your own skills.

Colour

White and clear crystals indicate that you need to sort out your priorities; blue suggests re-evaluating your own needs and patterns is the way forward; red indicates that you need to think about your work–life balance.

The Seventh House of Partnership

Ruling energy: Libra

Keywords

Relationship, partners, love affairs.

Meaning

If crystals fall in this house, you can be assured that a romantic relationship is a key influence in your reading, and you need to turn your attention towards it.

Colour

Pink crystals signify making a commitment; brown or black crystals suggest making changes to a relationship to make it work; green crystals suggest rethinking your relationship in order to create better balance and harmony.

The Eighth House of Sex, Death and Transformation
Ruling energy: Scorpio

KEYWORDS
Transformation, change, joint resources, intense feelings.

MEANING
You may need to accept that change is inevitable, or take an objective look at an intimate relationship.

COLOUR
Red, black or brown crystals reinforce the idea of change; clear, pink or yellow stones suggest it's time to pay attention to joint finances or property matters; green shows it's time to make a joint long-term decision.

The Ninth House of Philosophy and Adventure
Ruling energy: Sagittarius

KEYWORDS
Travel, adventure, wisdom, openness to new ideas.

MEANING
When crystals fall here, it shows you are about to undertake some form of voyage – either of the intellectual or physical kind.

Colour
Green or yellow crystals indicate that you will benefit from being open to new ideas and broadening your perspective on life; all other colours suggest it's time to get ready for a new adventure.

The Tenth House of Social Status
Ruling energy: Capricorn

Keywords
Ambition, career, integrity, self-belief, manifestation.

Meaning
Crystals falling here suggest you're ready to resolve any problem. They also indicate that things that have fallen apart are now coming together again. Your ambitions or career may be highlighted.

Colour
Black, red or green stones can reveal that your goals are attainable; clear, pink or yellow stones indicate you need to express your goals and show acceptance of other people's values.

The Eleventh House of Friendship
Ruling energy: Aquarius

Keywords
Social contacts, friends, environment, groups.

MEANING
Crystals falling in this segment reveal the influence of friends, the world around you, and the effect they have on you.

COLOUR
Pink crystals signal compassion will help you achieve your goals; blue that a calm environment will restore your soul; yellow suggests that communicating to a wider audience can bring you happiness.

The Twelfth House of the Unconscious

Ruling energy: Pisces

KEYWORDS
Reflection, intuition, imagination, ideals.

MEANING
Crystals falling here indicate that it's time to listen to your inner voice and trust yourself. Use your imagination or get creative with your dreams.

COLOUR
Blue, purple or clear crystals encourage you to listen to your intuition and follow your instincts; black, brown or red stones indicate that you should reflect before making a decision; yellow stones remind you your ideals are in question; and green stones show that you can use your imagination to make creative progress.

THE ZODIAC BOARD

Now that you have an understanding of the houses of the zodiac, you can start putting your knowledge into practice through divination. The zodiac divinatory board is divided into twelve equal segments, representing the twelve houses of the zodiac, and it can be used to give a broader, more all-encompassing reading.

You will need:

a large piece of paper and a pen or pencil (or a print-out of a ready-made zodiac circle)
a pouch or paper bag
12 crystals (include one of each colour from the list on page 100; the rest are for you to decide. It's best to use the same crystals each time to maintain their sacred divination usage and provide clarity for readings)

1. If you're creating a zodiac circle by hand, then either draw a large rough circle, use a compass, or grab your biggest dinner plate and trace round it.
2. Divide the circle into twelve equal segments by drawing six lines cutting through the middle of the circle.

There are two ways to cast crystals:

Shake and cast method

1. If you are using very small polished or tumbled stones, hold them in your hands, close your eyes, focus on your question and shake them like you would dice.
2. When you feel the moment is right, and have thought deeply enough about your intention, release the stones gently on to the board and let them fall as they will. Don't attempt to touch or move them, or you will devalue their energy and the reading.

One-at-a-time method

1. If you have larger crystals, focus on your issue, and then cast one crystal at a time on to your board. Keep your hand in the same position each time when casting – don't try to throw the crystal into an empty space or on a place on the board where you are keen for it to land! In fact, it's usually advised to close your eyes when casting, and if the crystal falls outside of the circle, there is an interpretation for this anyway.
2. Repeat the casting of each stone in your bag until you have finished.

Seeing how the crystals fall

1. Now look at how the crystals have fallen on the circle. Are they in groups? Are they more to the left, right, middle, top or bottom? Are they splayed out in all directions? Have any fallen beyond the edge of the circle? They way in which they have fallen will indicate which of the crystals is the most relevant to your question, and which you can ignore.

    - **Crystals that form a tight-knit group within the circle:** The houses where these crystals fall are of importance to the question, even if they cross over two houses. Both will be relevant.
    - **Crystals that touch each other:** The crystals' energies are personally important to the questioner, even if they are in different houses; both houses are influential and so are both of the stones.
    - **A group of crystals (whether close together or spaced widely apart) straddling in and out of the circle:** The crystals within the circumference are external influences in your current situation right now. The stones that lie outside the circle will become influential in a few weeks' time. The further out of the circle they are, the longer the time span.

- **Rogue crystals that fall outside the board:** These stones are less important right now. You can ignore them.
- **Any single crystal on the edge of the board, partly in, partly out:** This crystal indicates the type of influence that will be coming to you and then leaving again.
- **Any crystal – or cluster of crystals touching one another – that lies in the centre of the zodiac circle**: These are personal stone(s) for the questioner and should be interpreted as 'me now', or my current state of being – these are usually key to your reading.
- **Single crystals within the board:** These crystals are important to you right now as they reveal needs and influences you might not have considered.

2. You might find it helpful to keep a pen and paper handy to jot down a note for each of the different readings to begin with. Once you have decided which crystals to concentrate on and which to ignore, you can start your reading from the first house segment on the left, and work anti-clockwise round the circle (as a zodiac chart is read). This means you can eliminate some houses where there are no crystals, and crystals that are not in play, rather than jumping around the circle haphazardly.

3. Once you have worked your way around the chart, you can read the bigger story aloud or to yourself, and see where the main influences are in your reading, and what your story is telling you.

How to interpret the crystals in their zodiac house placements

1. Apart from the overall energy of crystals in any of the houses, read each crystal's individual specific energy to add more 'meat' to your 'story'. For example, if you have a lone ruby in the fourth house, which refers to your home and family, the ruby adds to the story with the words 'self-confidence and self-belief'. So my interpretation would be, 'You can confidently focus on your family life right now.'

Remember

Always relate the crystals' placements and energies to the question or issue posed to determine the influences you should be looking at and see what areas of your life these are coming from.

Chapter 12

Other Kinds of Crystal Divination

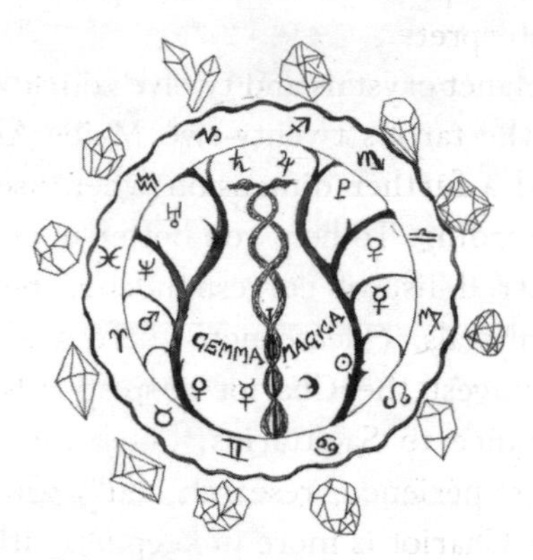

There are many other ways to use crystals for divination, including gazing into a crystal ball, known as scrying, using them as a support to a tarot reading, and divining for answers with a crystal pendulum. Of course, you can just hold a crystal of your choice before you and ask it a question. Whatever you do, crystals are here to help us discover our own truths.

Tarot and crystals

You may already be familiar with tarot, but don't worry if this is your first time delving into the cards. The classic Rider Waite Smith deck is perfect for beginners as all the pip cards (suit or Minor Arcana cards) are illustrated as well as the main picture cards, making it easier to understand and interpret.

The ten planet crystals and twelve zodiac crystals correspond to the tarot's twenty-two Major Arcana cards, and will add a further dimension when used simultaneously in a reading. To help you better understand, here is my preferred list of correspondence between tarot cards and crystals. (Please note there are many traditions that suggest the Chariot corresponds to Cancer, and Temperance to Sagittarius, but based on my own astrological experience, research and work with tarot, I believe the Chariot is more in keeping with Sagittarius and Cancer with Temperance. Ultimately, though, it's for you to decide.)

Card	Meaning	Planet/Zodiac	Significance	Crystal
0 – The Fool	Unlimited potential	Uranus	Freedom	Green aventurine
I – The Magician	Manifest action	Mercury	Magic	Sodalite
II – The High Priestess	Mystery	Moon	Receptivity	Selenite
III – The Empress	Creative abundance	Venus	Love	Rose quartz
IV – The Emperor	Authority	Aries	Organised action	Red carnelian
V – The Hierophant	Knowledge	Taurus	Respect	Emerald
VI – The Lovers	Love	Gemini	Choice	Citrine
VII – The Chariot	Self-belief	Sagittarius	Ambition	Turquoise
VIII – Strength	Courage	Leo	Power	Tiger's eye
IX – The Hermit	Discretion	Virgo	Discrimination	Peridot
X – The Wheel of Fortune	Destiny	Jupiter	Opportunity	Lapis lazuli
XI – Justice	Fairness	Libra	Compromise	Blue sapphire
XII – The Hanged Man	Paradox	Neptune	Transition	Celestite
XIII – Death	Change	Scorpio	Transformation	Obsidian
XIV – Temperance	Moderation	Cancer	Cooperation	Moonstone
XV – The Devil	Temptation	Capricorn	Materialism	Ruby
XVI – The Tower	The unexpected	Mars	Disruption	Bloodstone
XVII – The Star	Realisation	Aquarius	Inspiration	Amber
XVIII – The Moon	Illusion	Pisces	Vulnerability	Amethyst
XVIX – The Sun	Joy	Sun	Vitality	Sunstone
XX – Judgement	Liberation	Pluto	Rebirth	Black tourmaline
XXI – The World	Completion	Saturn	Accomplishment	Smoky quartz

Now, if you were to engage in a reading and draw the Devil, you can see that the Devil represents temptation, whether that signifies resistance to temptation, or being led astray by your desires (especially in the tarot's blockage position; a card placed in this position indicates the things or people that are stopping you from being true to yourself, or from achieving your goals).

The Devil is traditionally associated with Capricorn (the sign of ambition), and Capricorn with garnet or ruby. In divination, ruby represents, among other things, 'a feisty encounter'. So if we were to interpret this card combining all these little stories, we might say, 'A potent encounter will tempt you to further ambitions.' The ruby just adds a little more meat to the story than the tarot card would supply on its own.

For our purposes, as the tarot and its use with crystals would take more pages than I have available in this little book, here's how to place a crystal grid when performing tarot to protect you from psychic negativity, boost your intuitive powers and invoke incisive and empowering readings.

Crystal pentagram to reinforce readings

The pentagram is a well-known magical symbol, protecting, reinforcing and establishing your connection to the magic within you. This symbol connects you to cosmic archetypal knowledge, which you unconsciously intuit when you are divining the past, present and future.

Prepare this grid before you engage in any tarot reading.

You will need:

a candle
a piece of hematite
5 pieces of clear quartz
5 pieces of obsidian
5 pieces of citrine

1. Light your candle, and start by placing the piece of hematite to mark the centre of the pointed star.
2. Now place the five quartz crystals around the hematite to form the five points of the star: one to the north, one to the west, one to the east, one to south-west, one to the south-east.
3. Next place the five pieces of obsidian halfway on each axis between the hematite and the quartz.
4. Finally, place the five pieces of citrine between each of the five lines of the star.
5. To activate your grid, say:

'This pentagram of crystals strong
Will cast my tarot with no wrong,
With every card my choice be made
And all I know, it will not fade,
Take hematite to calm the flame,

Take crystals black, remove all fear,
Take citrine, quartz to stake my claim,
Then read the cards for futures clear.'

6. Leave the grid in a special part of your room where you do your tarot readings. If you need to remove it between readings, simply set it up again each time using this little ritual.

Scrying or crystal-ball reading

As we have seen, scrying was frequently performed by seers, magicians and occultists throughout history to foretell the future or divine the truth of a situation. The art of scrying requires you to look into a crystal ball and allow your mind to visualise shapes, forms, ideas and even faces, before interpreting what you see. The scientific viewpoint is that any reflective surface, such as a mirror or still water, is a suitable tool for projecting inner visions or images, but the crystal ball has always been the favourite due to its own mystical influences. It truly is a way to engage in different realms of consciousness, but you need to be quite practised at interpreting what you see. The best way to do this is to liken the images you glimpse to symbols, or weave them into a story that you can tell to yourself out loud, as we have done with other forms of divination.

Although authentic crystal spheres are quite costly, they are the best tools for scrying. You can find glass substitutes that are a lot cheaper, but the pure crystal ball vibrates to frequencies our imagination and intuition can access. Clear crystal is the best stone to use and is the perfect channel through which to connect the universe to your mind. It also has the power to calm and open you to your psychic world. You can also use large phantom quartz crystals with many facets or natural unshaped forms – or you can even opt for obsidian spheres and flat mirrors, which were used by ancient Native American peoples, as well as by Renaissance occultists such as sixteenth-century English astrologer Dr John Dee.

Scrying practice

Here is a way to practise scrying successfully.

You will need:

your chosen scrying crystal
calming essential oils
a piece of smoky quartz

1. Choose somewhere quiet and private for this practice, and make sure you have time to follow up with a grounding ritual afterwards.
2. Sit comfortably, making sure you are in a position that doesn't strain your body or your eyes. To improve your 'sight', you can place some dark fabric behind or under the crystal, or use subdued lighting.

3. Before you begin, close your eyes, settle into a serene state, and think carefully about what you are divining for. Whatever you are about to see will relate to your question, so make sure you have it firmly set in your mind before opening your eyes.
4. Open your eyes and stare or gaze at the crystal, and let your eyes go out of focus, rather than concentrating on one point. One way to practise this is to hold your finger up in front of your face, about a full arm's length away. Focus on the finger, then take your finger away and keep your eyes trained on the same focal point, as if you are focusing on nothing. It will seem as if you are looking around with your peripheral vision.
5. Keep repeating your question in your head. Don't keep going for longer than five minutes to begin with. Don't worry if you don't see anything the first few times you try this: it takes a bit of practice and patience. Eventually, though, visual images should occur. They may be foggy or shadowy, they may move or be still, but whatever you see is important. You may see shapes, mistiness, lights or symbols. Whatever you see, it is the influence not just of the crystal energy, but of your own imagination pulling images from your deeper unconscious into the tangible world.
6. Now it is time to interpret what you see. This is challenging, but it also stills the mind. You may be overwhelmed with shapes and images, so scribble

them down on a piece of paper, without taking your eyes off the ball. Reflect on what you have seen and how it can be interpreted in the light of your current situation.

7. After your practice, it's important to bring your mind back to ordinary functioning. You can leave your scrying crystal in a special place, cover it with a silk or cotton cloth, or surround it with a circle of protective or enlightening crystals, such as black tourmaline, smoky quartz or blue lace agate.
8. Run yourself a lovely bath (or shower) with essential oils such as lavender. Relax and immerse yourself in the water. Hold a piece of smoky quartz to ground your thoughts and continue your day.

How to use a crystal pendulum

Using a crystal pendulum is a fun way to get a quick 'yes' or 'no' answer to a straightforward question. Once you have worked out which swing of the pendulum means 'yes' to you, and which means 'no', take it with you wherever you go and call on it whenever you're in need of a helpful ally for making quick choices.

Form and colour

Crystal pendulums come in all shapes, sizes and stones. The best pendulum shapes are conical, pyramid, cylindrical or pointed and faceted crystals. The weight is important as the heavier stones produce a better momentum, and you can get to know the different swings quickly. Choose a crystal variety that has meaning for you: this could be your own zodiac crystal, or based on a personal experience.

When you ask a question, your unconscious mind connects to the universal energy, which then flows through you. The muscles of your hand holding the pendulum react to the vibrations of the earth without you realising it. This is known as the *ideomotor response*, where tiny, involuntary movements of the muscles in your arm and hand cause the pendulum to move and are amplified by the pendulum.

Some diviners use four potential responses to a question, but for our purposes, you're going to get used to using two to begin with: one for 'yes' and one for 'no'. Any other kind of swing means, 'Don't know – try again.'

The way you ask the question is just as important as the answer. There's no point asking a question that gives a choice, for example, 'Should I go to Spain or France for my holiday?' Nor is there any point asking a question that demands information, such as 'How can I make so-and-so fall in love with me?' But you could ask, 'Is it a good idea to go to Spain for my holiday?' or 'Will so-and-so fall in love with me?'

You can use your pendulum to help you locate lost items. To do this, you will have to go to various locations throughout the room or house, and at each spot ask, 'Is the object here?'

Step-by-step guide to using a crystal pendulum

You will need:

a crystal pendulum

1. Begin by sitting at a table and resting your elbow lightly on it. Make sure your legs aren't crossed, as this blocks the energy flow. Alternatively, stand with your arm extended from the elbow at waist height.
2. Hold the end of the thread or chain of your pendulum between your thumb and first finger, using a relaxed grip with very little pressure.
3. The pendulum should be hanging about 30cm (12in) in front of you. Make sure that your elbow is the only point of contact with the table. If you are standing, make sure your forearm is parallel with the ground.
4. Experiment to see whether a longer or shorter drop (the length of chain or thread attached to the pendulum) works best for you to get a good momentum when it swings. You can adjust this by twisting the thread or chain around your finger. Once you feel comfortable with the drop, grab the pendulum with your other hand to stop the movement.
5. Make sure that your body is relaxed and your mind

still. If you have never used a pendulum before, it can take a while before movements start, so be patient as you wait for its response. The pendulum may just move very slightly at first, but after a while, it can build up considerable movement. Remember, this is triggered by the vibrational forces of the universe affecting the tiny muscles in your arms and hand. The pendulum will work better if you remain open and trust in the universe and the energies flowing through you.

6. When you're ready, ask the first question. Choose one to which you know the answer is 'yes', for example, 'Is my name [X]?'
7. The pendulum will eventually begin to swing, either back and forth, left to right or round in a clockwise or anti-clockwise direction. Whichever direction it swings is probably the 'yes' swing, but it's a good idea to ask another question to which you know the answer is 'yes' to confirm this. If you get two different swings to the 'yes' answer, then keep going until you are sure you always have the same swing for 'yes'. Your body's connection to the universe will eventually cause the pendulum to settle into the natural swing for this answer.
8. Next, ask a question to which you know the answer is 'no'. Now let the pendulum swing until it moves in another direction. Again, you can confirm this 'no' swing by asking another 'no' question to which you know the answer.
9. Finally, ask a question that is logically meaningless,

such as 'Are two apples bigger than two pears?' The pendulum should then swing in a third way, to indicate 'don't know – try again'.

10. Once you've established your swings, you can now ask the pendulum questions to which you *don't* know the answers. This is when your unconscious starts to connect to the universal energy to generate the pendulum's response. Have fun asking questions, and be positive.

    Take care you don't project your own desires into the movement of the pendulum: here's how.

To avoid controlling the swings

We often unconsciously take control of the pendulum swings, and it is this power that can lead to wrong answers, or projected outcomes of our own desires. So it's important to learn to 'let go' of your mind while practising with a crystal pendulum.

1. Suspend the pendulum until it's motionless.
2. Out loud or in your head, tell the pendulum to move in a clockwise direction. Do not move your arm, wrist or hand.
3. Concentrate on the pendulum by staring at it, and thinking or saying, 'Clockwise, clockwise,' over and over again until the pendulum starts to move in that direction.
4. Stop the pendulum, then think hard about another direction, and you will find it again follows your thoughts.

5. Now free yourself from the power of your conscious mind by focusing on the pendulum without thinking about it. If you can't 'think of nothing', then repeat your chosen question like a mantra in your head, so that you are still receptive to the power of the universe, but are blocking out your causal mind. With practice, you'll learn to know the difference between intentionally causing the pendulum to move and a genuine response.

Pendulum dowsing over crystals and tarot cards

You can also dowse crystals and tarot cards themselves. For example, let's say you want to know if you should go to meet a new admirer or not. You can hold the pendulum over the crystal or tarot card, and ask, 'Is this the crystal/card that will give me the answer?' If the pendulum says, 'yes', then turn over the card or look at the crystal to interpret the meaning. If the pendulum says 'no', move on to the next card or crystal and repeat.

Tarot

Shuffle your tarot cards and place them facedown in a line in front of you. Hold the pendulum over each card, moving along the line until you get a 'yes' response. When you do, you will know this is the tarot card that will give you the best response to your question. Turn it over to interpret its message.

Crystals

Place your crystals in a pouch, then close your eyes and pull out several crystals. Place them on the table in front of you. Hold the pendulum over each, moving it over the crystals until you get a 'yes' response that will tell you this is the best crystal to interpret to answer your question. (To avoid projecting a 'yes' swing over your preferred crystal, cover the crystals with a cloth before you open your eyes.)

Accepting the answer

If the answer is not the one you had hoped for, question what your motives were for asking the question in the first place. And, as with any form of divination, whether you are dowsing, scrying, or using tarot or oracle crystals, the magic of the universe will start to work on your behalf, if you let it.

We have come to the end of this little book of crystal magic, but the magic of crystals is infinite. There is always more to learn, more to treasure and more crystals to befriend. So enjoy and look after your lovely stones, and they will reward you with their care in return.

Last words

The Serbian-American inventor and electrical engineer Nikola Tesla is believed to have said: 'In a crystal, we have clear evidence of a formative life principle, and though we cannot understand the life of a crystal, it is nonetheless a living being.' These living beings were forced into the upper world from their underworld beginnings, and though we cannot understand their atomic chattering, we can learn to understand how they speak to us on some subtle, symbolic or magical level. It seems they will befriend us and try to make their home with us if we open our minds, spirits and souls to their mystery, and respect their ancient heritage.

Write this final verse on a piece of paper. Place your favourite crystal or wild stone on the paper, then recite the verse aloud and cast the little spell at the end. You and the stone will be bonded forever on your magical journey.

'How many moons have you seen, and when?
What did they tell you about now and then?
Did you have rubies that charmed another?
Did you have snake-stones to curse a lover?
Did you return to a grove in your sleep
Where all was stillness and love could be reaped?

Or did you wait for another such night
To light up your candle and set all things right?
So take up your crystal, anoint it with oil,
Hold to your forehead and whisper this now,
"By the light of the moon I am free of the past
And blessed by the sun when each new spell
is cast."'"

Glossary of crystals and their properties

Amber: protection, detoxification, discovery, positivity

Amethyst: generosity, spiritual clarity, connection, calm

Aquamarine: intuition, relaxation, inner harmony, balance

Azurite: cosmic connection, intuitive awareness, sacred wisdom

Black tourmaline: protection, security, personal power

Bloodstone: courage, strength, success, motivation, action

Blue lace agate: clarity, focus, self-awareness, gentleness, peace

Celestite: telepathy, intuition, compassion, spiritual connection

Citrine: abundance, success, new beginnings, self-expression, happiness

Clear quartz: activation, focus, clarity, enlightenment, reinforcement

Emerald: wisdom, abundance, strength, loyalty, honesty, acceptance

Fire agate: charisma, passion, desire, motivation, success
Garnet: willpower, love, creativity, strength, fidelity, bonding
Goldstone: wealth, charisma, self-empowerment
Green aventurine: opportunity, change, free-spiritedness, radical breakthrough
Green jade: good luck, friendship, wisdom, fresh beginnings
Green tourmaline: abundance, prosperity, change
Hematite: grounding, protection, banishment of negativity
Kyanite: spiritual truth, acceptance, psychic power, self-awareness
Labradorite: psychic awareness, altered states of consciousness
Lapis lazuli: adventure, self-belief, inspiration, wisdom, conviction, truth
Malachite: stability, self-belief, emotional balance, grounding, protection
Moonstone: peace, protection, giving, self-understanding, belonging
Obsidian: transformation, control, protection, release from fear
Onyx: integrity, clarity of mind, truth
Opal: imagination, spontaneity, creativity, progress, diversity
Peridot: awakening, focus, self-reliance, adaptability, stress reduction

Phantom quartz: clarity, inspiration, illumination, enlightenment

Red carnelian: success, enterprise, determination, direction, self-value

Rhodochrosite: spontaneity, passion, unconditional love

Rose quartz: emotional healing, self-love, love, beauty, fulfilment, romance

Ruby: abundance, invincibility, wealth, power, desire, security, passion

Sapphire (blue): harmony, good fortune, fidelity, self-realisation

Selenite: intuition, security, fertility, instinct, clarity, serenity

Smoky quartz: ambition, determination, protection, manifestation, integrity

Sodalite: connection, flexibility, communication, transition, negotiation

Sunstone: joy, strength, prosperity, willpower, vitality

Tiger's eye: confidence, success, ardour, good luck, power, opportunity

Topaz: self-realisation, spiritual connection, insight, foresight

Turquoise: optimism, good luck, safety, wisdom, self-assurance

Glossary of correspondences

Here you will find suggested ingredients and other sacred resources for use in your magic work. Some are required for the spells in this book, while others can be used to create your own rituals and charms. It's also important to stress that working with deities and invoking their help to connect to the spiritual world around you is a crucial aspect of magic work. If you are unfamiliar with the deities referenced in this book, why not take some time to research and appreciate their spiritual traditions?

This glossary has been categorised by theme to make it as user-friendly as possible. For example, if you are in need of abundant ideas, you would choose ingredients in the associated list: you might set up a meditation altar in your sacred garden and ask the Hindu god Ganesha for positive thoughts and good luck; you could light a red candle, place a piece of malachite before the candle and drop a little patchouli oil on the crystal while repeating a charm. If you wish, you can also mix and match ingredients to reinforce various elements of your ritual or charm. But most of all, take pleasure and delight in the resources that Mother Nature offers you with her open arms.

Love and relationships

Deities to invoke for love and relationships

Áine (Celtic)
Aphrodite (Greek)
Eros (Greek)
Freyja (Norse)
Hathor (Egyptian)
Inanna (Sumerian)
Rati (Hindu)
Venus (Roman)

Botanicals for love and relationships

basil
hawthorn
jasmine
lavender
lily
lemon verbena
orchid
rose
rosemary
wormwood

Colours for love and relationships

pink (romance, attraction)
red (passion, sexuality)
white (purity, commitment)
yellow (friendship)

Crystals and precious stones for love and relationships

emerald
garnet
kunzite
lepidolite
red carnelian
red jasper
rose quartz
ruby

Essential oils for love and relationships

jasmine
lotus
patchouli
rose
ylang ylang

Prosperity and abundance

Deities to invoke for prosperity and abundance

Agathodaimon (Greek)
Ebisu (Japanese)
Fortuna (Roman)
Ganesha (Hindu)
Lakshmi (Hindu)
Vesunna (Celtic Gaul)

Botanicals for prosperity and abundance

clover
elderflower
garlic
jade plant
oak
pine
thyme

Colours for prosperity and abundance

black (reinforcement)
brown (strength)
red (empowerment)

Crystals and precious stones for prosperity and abundance

amazonite
citrine
emerald
green jade
malachite
pyrite

Essential oils for prosperity and abundance

bergamot
frankincense
ginger
oud
patchouli

Success and self-empowerment

Deities to invoke for success and self-empowerment

Apollo (Greek)
Artemis (Greek)
Brigid (Celtic)
Cernunnos (Celtic)
Durga (Hindu)
Indra (Hindu)
Isis (Egyptian)
Zeus (Greek)

Botanicals for success and self-empowerment

angelica
bay leaf
birch
ficus
olive leaf
sage
thyme

Colours for success and self-empowerment

black (integrity)
brown (conviction)
green (manifestation)
red (self-belief)

Crystals and precious stones for success and self-empowerment

ametrine
carnelian
jet
obsidian
sunstone

Essential oils for success and self-empowerment

cedarwood
eucalyptus
oud
vetiver

Spiritual growth

Deities to invoke for spiritual growth

Arianrhod (Celtic)
Artemis (Greek)
Hecate (Greek)
Horus (Egyptian)
Selene (Greek)

Botanicals for spiritual growth

ash tree
hibiscus
honeysuckle
lavender
lotus

poppy
water lily

Colours for spiritual growth

blue (intuition)
purple (spiritual awareness)
turquoise (compassion)
white (soul/divine connection)

Crystals and precious stones for spiritual growth

clear quartz
fluorite
labradorite
lapis lazuli
moonstone
turquoise

Essential oils for spiritual growth

cedarwood
clove
cypress
sandalwood

About the Author

Sarah Bartlett is a professional astrologer and author of internationally bestselling books such as *The Little Book of Magic* series, *The Tarot Bible*, *The Witch's Spellbook*, *The Secrets of the Universe in 100 Symbols* and *National Geographic Guide to the World's Supernatural Places*. Sarah practises natural magic, tarot, astrology and other esoteric arts in the heart of the countryside.